WJEC GCSE HISTORY

# Russia in Transition 1914–1924

John Wright, Steve Waugh
Editor: R. Paul Evans

For Ella Zoe Smith

Hachette UK's policy is to use papers that are natural, renewable and recyclable products and made from wood grown in sustainable forests. The logging and manufacturing processes are expected to conform to the environmental regulations of the country of origin.

Orders: please contact Bookpoint Ltd, 130 Milton Park, Abingdon, Oxon OX14 4SB. Telephone: (44) 01235 827720. Fax: (44) 01235 400454. Lines are open 9.00–5.00, Monday to Saturday, with a 24-hour message answering service. Visit our website at www.hoddereducation.co.uk


First published in 2012 by
Hodder Education,
An Hachette UK Company
338 Euston Road
London NW1 3BH

Impression number 5 4 3 2 1
Year 2016 2015 2014 2013 2012



Cover photos *l* Tsar Nicholas II of Russia © The Print Collector/Corbis; *r* Portrait of Lenin © Bettmann/Corbis
Illustrations by Gray Publishing
Typeset in 11pt Minion and produced by Gray Publishing, Tunbridge Wells, Kent
Printed in Italy

A catalogue record for this title is available from the British Library

ISBN: 978 1444 156294

The Publishers would like to thank the following for permission to reproduce copyright material:

**Photo credits**

**pp. 7, p. 10 *l*, *r*** David King Collection; **p. 11** RIA Novosti; **p. 12** Getty Images; **p. 14** David King Collection; **p. 19** Getty Images; **p. 22** Mary Evans Picture Library/Alexander Meledin; **pp. 25, 29** David King Collection; **p. 30** Bettmann/CORBIS; **p. 31** Popperfoto/Getty Images; **pp. 32, 34, 35** David King Collection; **p. 36** AFP/Getty Images; **p. 38 *both*** Getty Images; **p. 41** David King Collection; **p. 46** Hulton-Deutsch Collection/CORBIS; **p. 50** David King Collection; **p. 51** Alinari/The Bridgeman Art Library; **p. 53** CORBIS; **p. 56** Hulton-Deutsch Collection/CORBIS; **pp. 58, 64, 65** David King Collection; **p. 66** Hoover Institute; **p. 68** Private Collection/ Archives Charmet/The Bridgeman Art Library; **p. 69** David King Collection; **p. 72** Getty Images; **p. 73** Robert Hunt Library/Mary Evans; **p. 74** Hoover Institute; **p. 75** www.redavantgarde.com; **p. 78** Robert Hunt Library/Mary Evans; **p. 82 *t*** David King Collection; **p. 82 *b*** Hulton-Deutsch Collection/ CORBIS; **p. 84** Central Naval Museum, St. Petersburg, Russia/The Bridgeman Art Library; **p. 86** David King Collection; **p. 89** Getty Images; **p. 91** David King Collection; **p. 97** Getty Images; **p. 98** David King Collection; **pp. 99, 104** Getty Images; **p. 105** Private Collection/Peter Newark Pictures/The Bridgeman Art Library; **p. 106 *tl*** David King Collection; **p. 106 *ml*** Underwood & Underwood/Corbis; **p. 106 *bl*, *tr*** Bettmann/ CORBIS; **p. 106 *br*** Hulton-Deutsch Collection/CORBIS; **p. 108** David King Collection; **p. 109 *l*** Hulton-Deutsch Collection/CORBIS; **p. 109 *r*** David King Collection; **p. 110** Hulton-Deutsch Collection/CORBIS; **p. 113 *l*** David King Collection; **p. 113 *r*** Mary Evans Picture Library.

**Acknowledgements**

**p. 59** C. Baker, *Russia 1917–1945*, Heinemann, 1990; **p. 61** J. Brooman, *Russia in War and Revolution*, Pearson, 1986; **p. 83, 84, 94 *l*, 96 *l*, *r*** C. Corin and T. Fiehn, *Communist Russia Under Lenin and Stalin*, Hodder Education, 2002, reproduced by permission of Hodder Education; **p. 80** J. Daborn, *Russia: Revolution and Counter-Revolution 1917–24*, Cambridge University Press, 1991; **p. 89** T. Downey, *Russia and the USSR 1900–1995*, Oxford University Press, 1996; **p. 8, 18 *r*, 19, 20, 24 *l*, *r*, 28 bl, 36, 111** T. Fiehn, *Discovering the Past for GCSE: Russia and the USSR*, Hodder Education, 1996, reproduced by permission of Hodder Education; **p. 67, 104, 107 *tr*, 112 *bl*** O. Figes *A People's Tragedy*, Pimlico, 1996; **p. 103** *Guardian News and Media*; **p. 65 *br*** H. Hist and C. Baker, *Russia 1917–45*, Heinemann, 1990; **p. 57 *br*** N. Kelly, *Russia and the USSR 1905–56*, Heinemann, 1996; **p. 87 *tl*** J. Laver, *Russia and the USSR 1905–56*, Hodder Education, 1997; **p. 26, 39 *l*, 46 *r*** M. Lynch, *Reaction and Revolution: Russia, 1894–1924*, Hodder Education, 2005; **p. 75 *r*** H. MacDonald, *Russia and the USSR*, Longman, 2001; **p. 85 *r*** www.marxists.org/Marxists Internet Archive; **p. 18 *l*, 35 *ml*, 112 *tl*** T. Pimlott, *Russian Revolution*, Macmillan, 1985; **p. 17 *tl*, 28 *tl*** J. Robottom, *Russia in Change 1870–1945*, Pearson, 1984; **p. 45 *bl*, 46 *bl*, 47, 98** R. Radway, *Russia and the USSR 1900–45*, Thornes 1996; **p. 43 *br*** Leonard Schapiro, *The Communist Party of the Soviet Union*, Eyre & Spottiswoode, 1960; **p. 87 *r*** V. Serge, *From Lenin to Stalin*, Pathfinder, 2005; **p. 35 *tl*, 52 *r*, 75 *l*** V. Serge, *Memoirs of a Revolutionary 1901–41*, Oxford University Press, 1967; **p. 108** R. Seth, *Leon Trotsky: The Eternal Rebel*, Dobson, 1967; **p. 14, 23, 33, 39 *r*, 43 *tr*, 45 *tl*, *ml*** J. Simkin, *The Russian Revolution*, Spartacus, 1986; **p. 57 *l*, 94 *br*** F.W. Stacey, *Lenin and the Russian Revolutions*, Hodder, 1968; **p. 37** A. J. P. Taylor, *Revolutions and Revolutionaries*, Oxford University Press, 1980; **p. 112 *ml*, 114 *l*** *Times Newspapers*; **p. 6** Leon Trotsky, *The History of the Russian Revolution*, Haymarket, 2007; **p. 110** A. Ulam, *Lenin and the Bolsheviks*, Secker & Warburg, 1969; **p. 71, 72, 78, 87 *bl*** B. Walsh, *Modern World History*, Hodder Murray, 1996, reproduced by permission of Hodder Education; **p. 11, 12 *tl*, *bl*** S. Waugh and J. Wright, *Russia 1917–1939*, Hodder, 2009; **p. 107 *l*** S. Waugh and J. Wright, *The Russian Revolution and Soviet Union 1910–1991*, Hodder Education, 2006; **p. 64, 65 *tr*, 73, 81** A. White, *Russia and the USSR*, Collins, 1994; **pp. 4–5** WJEC; **p. 76** A. Wood, *The Russian Revolution*, Longman 1986.

Every effort has been made to trace all copyright holders, but if any have been inadvertently overlooked the Publishers will be pleased to make the necessary arrangements at the first opportunity.

# INTRODUCTION

## About the course

During this course you must study four units:

- Two studies in depth (Units 1 and 2).
- One study in outline (Unit 3).
- An investigation into an issue of historical debate or controversy (Unit 4).

These are assessed through three examination papers and one controlled assessment:

- For Units 1 and 2 you have two hours to answer questions on the two depth studies you have studied.
- For Unit 3 you have one hour and fifteen minutes to answer questions on the outline study you have studied.
- In the internal assessment (Unit 4) you have to complete a task under controlled conditions in the classroom.

## About the book

This book covers the depth study 'Russia in Transition, 1914–1924' (which is either Unit 1 or Unit 2). It is divided into three sections, each with three chapters.

- **Section A** examines the causes and impact of the Revolutions of 1917, including what caused each of the revolutions, the key features of the February Revolution, Dual Power and the October Revolution, the ending of the war and the establishment of Communist rule.
- **Section B** concentrates on the causes and impact of the Civil War, 1918–21, including the main causes of the Civil War, the two sides in the war and reasons for the victory of the Reds.
- **Section C** explains the development of the Communist state 1921–24 including the key features of the New Economic Policy, how successful Lenin was in establishing a Communist state and his legacy in Russia.

### Each chapter

- contains activities – some develop the historical skills you will need, others are exam-style questions that give you the opportunity to practise exam skills. Exam-style questions are highlighted in blue
- gives step-by-step guidance, model answers and advice on how to answer particular question types that appear in the examination for Units 1 and 2.

## About Units 1 and 2

The examinations for Units 1 and 2 test two main areas:

- knowledge and understanding of the key developments in each of the three sections for the depth study you have studied
- the ability to answer a range of questions testing different skills.

The examinations will include a mix of written and illustrative sources:

- Written sources could include extracts from diaries, speeches, letters, poems, songs, biographies, autobiographies, memoirs, newspapers, modern history textbooks, the views of historians, or information from the internet.
- Illustrations could include photographs, posters, cartoons or paintings.

You will have to answer the following types of approved questions which ask you to demonstrate different source and communication skills:

- Comprehension of a visual source – asking you to select information from the source.
- Comprehension of a source linked to the recall of your own knowledge – asking you to explain what is in the source and place it within its historical context.
- The analysis of a source, supported with the use of your own knowledge – asking you to make a judgement on the extent to which a source supports a particular view.
- Utility – asking you to evaluate how useful a source is.
- Cross-referencing two sources to evaluate different viewpoints or interpretation.
- Describe – asking you to give a detailed description, usually of the key events in a period.
- Explanation – asking you to explain why something happened during this period.
- Importance/significance – asking you to analyse and evaluate the contribution of an event, personality or issue.
- Essay writing – asking you to assess the importance of particular developments and make a judgement.

## Example questions

On pages 4–5 are examples of approved questions for Units 1 and 2 (without the sources). You will be given step-by-step guidance throughout each part of the book on how to best approach and answer these questions.

# Units 1 and 2

## Question 1

a What does Source A tell you about the role of Lenin?
*(2 marks)*

b Use the information in Source B and your own knowledge to explain why the Provisional Government faced problems in the autumn of 1917.
*(4 marks)*

c How far does Source C support the view that the Bolshevik seizure of power had the widespread support of the workers in the cities?
*(5 marks)*

d How useful is Source D to a historian studying support for the Bolsheviks?
*(6 marks)*

e Why do Sources E and F have different views about who led the Bolsheviks?
*(8 marks)*

This is a **comprehension** of a **visual source** question asking you to select information from the source.

This is a **comprehension** of a **source** question, asking you to explain what is referred to in the source and to place it within its historical context through the inclusion of your own knowledge.

This question asks you to **analyse** a source and **make a judgement** on the extent to which it supports a particular view.

This is a **utility** question. You must decide how useful a source is to a historian undertaking an enquiry.

This is a question about differing viewpoints of a historical issue which requires you to **cross-reference** two viewpoints or interpretations, comparing their contents and the authors.

**Question 2** (this advice applies for examinations from summer 2013 onwards)

a Describe what happened to the tsar and his family in 1918.
*(4 marks)*

b Explain why the Civil War began in Russia in 1918.
*(5 marks)*

c How important was the policy of War Communism?
*(6 marks)*

**Question 3** (this advice applies for examinations from summer 2013 onwards)

Had Lenin succeeded in establishing a strong Communist state by 1924?
*(10 marks & 3 marks for SPaG)*

*In your answer you should:*

- *discuss the measures that helped Lenin create a strong Communist state*
- *discuss any measures that show the Communist state was not so strong.*

This is a **describe** question which tests your knowledge and understanding of a key feature.

This is an **explanation** question, asking you to explain why something happened during this period.

This is an **evaluation** question, expecting you to discuss why a person, event or development was significant or important.

This is an **essay** question. You are required to use your own knowledge to debate an issue. You should also provide a judgement upon the set question. Your answer will also be awarded marks for good spelling, punctuation and grammar (SPaG).

**Source A** From *The History of the Russian Revolution*, by Leon Trotsky, one of the leading revolutionaries of the time

*One half of the workers of Petrograd are on strike on 24 February. The workers come to the factories in the morning; instead of going to work they hold meetings; then begin the processions towards the centre. The slogan 'Bread' is drowned out by louder slogans: 'Down with the* ***autocracy****!' 'Down with the war!' Around the barracks and lines of soldiers stood groups of working men and women exchanging friendly words with the army men.*

This section examines the causes and consequences of the two revolutions in Russia in 1917. The period from 1914 to 1917 was one of turmoil and chaos for Russia and was dominated by the First World War and then revolution (see Source A). Russia entered the war with great optimism but, after many defeats coupled with social, economic and political problems, the Romanov monarchy was overthrown in February 1917.

The monarchy's replacement, the **Provisional Government**, seemed to promise a new era of reform. However, in October 1917, the new government fell to the **Bolsheviks** and this introduced the era of communism to Russia.

Each chapter explains a key issue and examines important lines of enquiry as outlined opposite.

**Chapter 1:** What were the causes of the Revolutions of 1917?

- What were the key features of Russian politics, economy and society?
- Why did opposition to Tsar Nicholas II grow in the years before 1914?
- What was Russia's experience in the First World War?
- Why did Russia suffer so many defeats and what were the effects?

**Chapter 2**: What were the main developments during the Bolshevik seizure of power?

- Why was there a revolution in Russia in February 1917?
- Why did rivalry emerge between the Provisional Government and the Petrograd **Soviet**?
- How did the Bolsheviks seize power in October 1917?
- What were the main events of the Bolshevik Revolution?
- Why were the Bolsheviks successful?

**Chapter 3:** What were the consequences of the Revolutions of 1917?

- How did the Bolsheviks establish the new Communist state?
- Why was the Treaty of Brest-Litovsk important?

# What were the causes of the Revolutions of 1917?

Russia at the beginning of the twentieth century was a vast empire covering one-sixth of the world's surface. It was ruled by Tsar Nicholas II, who faced a number of political, economic, social, religious and geographical problems. By 1900, there were many people within Russia who opposed the tsar and it was at this time that political parties began to emerge. What must be remembered is that although there was opposition to the tsarist system, most people did not seek to replace Nicholas II. They simply wanted reform within the existing system and there was quite a reservoir of goodwill towards Nicholas. However, this reservoir began to run dry when he failed to introduce long-lasting reforms in the years leading up to 1917. By February 1917, Nicholas had been forced to give up his throne. Russia was no longer a monarchy.

This chapter answers the following questions:

- What were the key features of Russian politics, economy and society?
- Why did opposition to Tsar Nicholas II grow in the years before 1914?
- What was Russia's experience in the First World War?
- Why did Russia suffer so many defeats and what were the effects?

**Source A** Cartoon showing the different groups in Russia at the beginning of the twentieth century

## TASKS

Study Source A.

**1** Each numbered arrow represents a different class or group in Russian society. Try to identify each one.

**2** What can you learn from Source A about Russian society in the early twentieth century?

### Examination guidance

Throughout this chapter you will be given the opportunity to practise different exam-style questions and detailed guidance on how to answer a comprehension of a visual source question. This is worth 2 marks.

# What were the key features of Russian politics, economy and society?

## How was Russia governed?

Russia was an autocracy with all the power in the hands of the tsar. The tsar believed that he had a divine right to rule, that is, he had been chosen by God. This meant he could do whatever he liked without having to consult his people. There was no parliament to represent the people's views.

The tsar did have a council of ministers that ran the various government departments, but it could not make important decisions. There were thousands of civil servants, such as tax collectors, who carried out the day-to-day work of government. They were generally poorly paid, so this encouraged bribery and corruption.

The Russian people had little freedom. All unions of workers and strikes were forbidden, and newspapers and books were censored by the government. The tsar was determined to suppress all opposition through the *Okhrana*, his secret police. The secret police used spies and agents to root out anyone who was against the tsar and his system of government. Such opponents could be imprisoned without trial or exiled to far-off Siberia.

**Source A** Extract from an open letter from Leo Tolstoy, a Russian novelist, who wrote to Tsar Nicholas II about Russia in the early twentieth century

> *A third of the whole of Russia lives under police surveillance. The army of the police, both regular and secret, is continually growing in numbers. The prisons are overcrowded with thousands of convicts and political prisoners. Censorship has reached its highest level since the 1840s. In all cities ... soldiers are ... equipped with live ammunition to be sent out against the people.*

**Source B** The Russian Empire in the early twentieth century

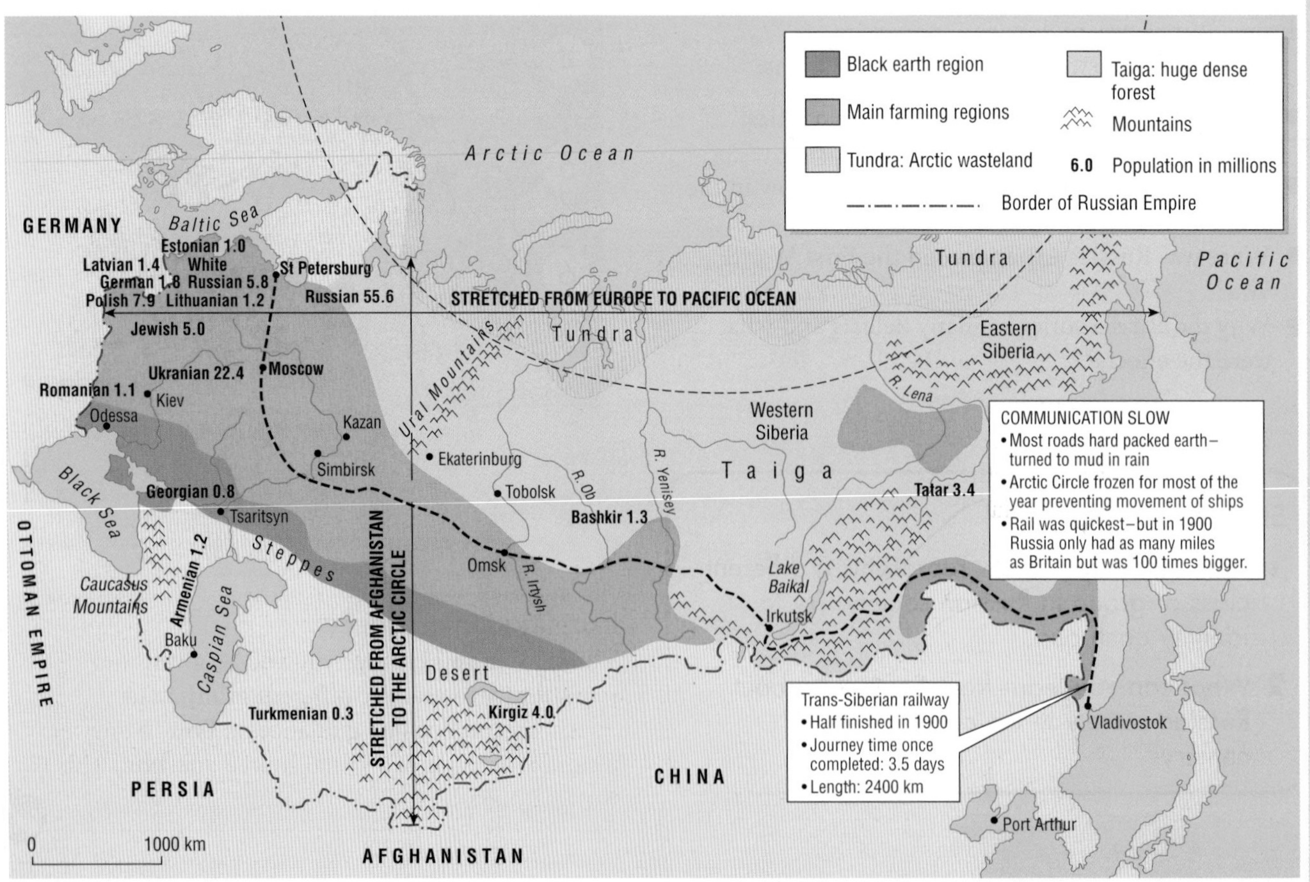

## Why was Russia difficult to govern?

Source B on page 8 shows some of the geographical reasons why the size of the Russian Empire made it difficult to govern.

It was also difficult to rule because of the many different peoples or ethnic groups in the empire. The population of Russia in 1914 was about 130 million and was made up of more than twenty different ethnic groups. For six people out of every ten, Russian was a foreign language. Many of these peoples resented being part of the empire, especially as the rulers of Russia carried out a policy of **Russification**. This meant making non-Russians speak Russian, wear Russian clothes and follow Russian customs.

## The Orthodox Church

About 70 per cent of the population were members of the official **Orthodox Church**. The Church was very closely linked to the tsar and supported his way of ruling. It taught that the tsar was the head of the country and the Church – in other words, that he was God's chosen representative on earth.

The Orthodox Church was unpopular because large minorities belonged to other Churches and religions, and they resented its power and privileges. For example, nine per cent of the population was Roman Catholic and eleven per cent Muslim. Also, the Orthodox Church was very wealthy, which contrasted greatly with the poor lifestyle of the majority of Russian people.

## The Russian economy

Russian agriculture was backward. Extensive **tundra**, forest and desert meant that not all the land was suitable for agriculture and the best arable farming was in the 'Black earth region' (see Source B on page 8). Old-fashioned farming methods resulted in low food production and frequent famines.

Even though Russia was rich in oil and minerals, industrialisation did not happen until the end of the nineteenth century (much later than some other European countries, such as Britain and Germany). Considering Russia's size and resources, its manufacturing output was still very low at the beginning of the twentieth century. Its size and undeveloped system of roads and railways, together with the absence of an effective banking system, all restricted the growth of industry.

One of the tsar's ministers, Count Sergei Witte, who was minister of finance from 1893 to 1903, set himself the task of modernising the Russian economy. He invited foreign experts and workers to advise on industrial planning and techniques. His reforms did stimulate industrial growth as can be seen in Source C.

**Source C** Russia's annual industrial and agricultural production from 1890 to 1913

| Year | Annual production (millions of tonnes) | | | |
|---|---|---|---|---|
| | Coal | Pig iron | Oil | Grain* |
| 1890 | 5.9 | 0.89 | 3.9 | 36 |
| 1900 | 16.1 | 2.66 | 10.2 | 56 |
| 1910 | 26.8 | 2.99 | 9.4 | 74 |
| 1913 | 35.4 | 4.12 | 9.1 | 90 |

*European Russia only.

By the outbreak of the First World War, Russia was experiencing a rapid growth in industry due to:

- an increase in the output of coal in the Ukraine
- an increase in the output of oil in the Caucasus
- deliberate government policy.

### TASKS

1. Using Source B, suggest reasons why the size of the Russian Empire made it so difficult to govern.
2. Why do you think the many non-Russian groups in the Russian Empire were known as the 'subject' nationalities?
3. What does Source A tell you about how Russia was ruled in the early twentieth century?
4. Explain why Russia was so difficult to govern. (For guidance on answering this type of question, see page 90.)
5. Source A gives only an extract from Tolstoy's letter. Using information from this section, add another paragraph to his letter about other reasons for discontent in Russia.
6. Examine Source C. Describe the key features of Russian industrial development in the period shown.

## Russian society

Russia also experienced the social problems that normally go with early and rapid industrialisation. Many peasants moved to the towns and cities to work in industry. This brought problems with living and working conditions.

As you have seen in Source A on page 7, Russian society was divided into various classes or groups. The vast majority of the people were poor peasants. At the other end of the scale, at the top, was the aristocracy.

### The aristocracy and middle class

The aristocracy made up just over one per cent of the population and yet they owned almost one-quarter of all the land. Some were extremely rich, with lavish homes in the countryside, a second home in a town or city and many servants. By 1914, Russia had a middle class whose numbers were increasing due to the development of industry. It included bankers, merchants and factory owners. Many made fortunes from government contracts and loans and had a very pleasant lifestyle; eating out at expensive restaurants and frequently going to the theatre or ballet.

**Source D** A dinner party in the palace of Countess Yelisaveta Shuvalova in St Petersburg in 1900

### The peasants

The biggest, and poorest group, were the peasants. About 80 per cent of Russian people were peasants in the years before 1917. For most, life was very hard. They lived in very poor conditions and survived on a staple diet of rye bread, porridge and cabbage soup. When the harvests were poor, there was starvation and disease. They had a life expectancy of less than 40 years, with many dying from typhus and diphtheria.

Many peasants felt bitter towards the aristocracy and their generally extravagant lifestyle. The nobles had kept most of the land when serfdom ended in 1861 and peasants resented having to work on nobles' estates to earn money. A population growth of 50 per cent between 1860 and 1897 brought greater competition for land and even smaller peasant plots.

**Source E** A photograph of a starving peasant family

**TASKS**

**7** Study Sources D and E. How could these photographs have been used to increase opposition to Tsar Nicholas II?

**8** What does Source E show you about living conditions of Russian peasants before 1917? (For guidance on answering this type of question, see page 22.)

## Town workers

The most rapidly increasing group were the new workers in industry in the towns and cities. Large numbers of peasants had flocked to the towns and cities to work in industry. Their conditions were terrible. Workers lived in overcrowded slums and ate cheap black bread, cabbage soup and wheat porridge. In industrial centres away from the cities, workers often lived in barracks next to the factory and slept in filthy, overcrowded dormitories. They earned low wages, worked long hours and were forbidden to form trade unions to fight for better conditions. Protests or strikes were crushed, often with great brutality, by the police or army.

**Source F** A typical flat in St Petersburg for workers in industry in the late 1890s

**Source G** From *The Story of My Life*, by Father Gapon written in 1905. Gapon was a priest who organised a trade union to help workers

*The workers receive terrible wages, and generally live in overcrowded conditions. The normal working day is eleven and a half hours not including meal times. But manufacturers have received permission to use overtime. This makes the average day longer than that allowed by the law – fifteen or sixteen hours.*

## TASKS

**9** Look again at the cartoon showing the different groups in Russian society (Source A, page 7).

- **a** Do your own sketch to show these different groups.
- **b** Annotate your sketch with key words to show the main features of each group.

**10** How useful is Source F to a historian studying life in Russia at this time? (For guidance on answering this type of question, see pages 59–60.)

**11** How far does Source G support the view that many Russian workers were exploited at the beginning of the twentieth century? (For guidance on answering this type of question, see pages 48–49.)

**12** Describe the lifestyle of people living in Russia in the early twentieth century. (For guidance on answering this type of question, see page 79.)

**13** Make a copy of the following table and use the sources and information on this page and pages 8–10 to complete it.

- In the second column give a brief explanation for their discontent.
- In the third column explain what you think the tsar should do to reduce or remove this discontent.

| | Why discontented? | What the tsar should do |
|---|---|---|
| Subject nationalities | | |
| Peasants | | |
| Town workers | | |

# Why did opposition to Tsar Nicholas II grow in the years before 1914?

## The character of Tsar Nicholas II

The system of autocracy only worked if the tsar was strong and able to control the government and different nationalities of the vast Russian Empire.

Nicholas II insisted on governing as an autocrat. He and his wife, the Tsarina Alexandra, believed that they had been chosen by God to rule and that no one had the right to challenge them. He was ignorant of the nature and extent of opposition to tsarist rule and refused to share power. It was once said that 'The two most important people in Russia are Tsar Nicholas II and the last person to whom he had spoken'.

Although a devoted husband and father, his family was not particularly happy. His only son and heir, Alexis, suffered from an incurable blood disease known as **haemophilia** and was likely to die young.

**Source A** Nicholas II speaking to an adviser on becoming tsar in 1894

*What is going to happen to me? I am not prepared to be tsar. I never wanted to become one. I know nothing of the business of ruling. I have no idea of even how to talk to ministers.*

**Source B** Extract from the diary of the tsar's sister, the Grand Duchess Olga

*He had intelligence ... faith and courage but he was ... ignorant about governmental matters. Nicky had been trained as a soldier. He had not been taught statesmanship and ... was not a statesman.*

**Source C** Nicholas II and his family

## TASKS

1 Study Sources A and B. What impression do you have of Nicholas from these sources? Explain your answer.

2 What does Source C tell you about Tsar Nicholas II?
(For guidance on answering this type of question, see page 22.)

3 Explain what was meant when it was said that the 'second most important person in Russia was the last person to whom Nicholas II had spoken'.

## The growth of opposition to Tsar Nicholas II before 1917

In the years before 1917, there was increasing opposition to Nicholas II for several reasons.

### Reasons for the growth of opposition to Nicholas II

**'Bloody Sunday', 22 January 1905**
This was a peaceful march by around 200,000 people to the tsar's Winter Palace, led by Father Gapon, to petition for better working conditions. However, the tsar was not in his palace and the soldiers panicked. They fired on the crowd, killing hundreds and wounding thousands.

**Source D** From a letter by an American diplomat in the Russian city of Odessa. He was writing about the consequences of Bloody Sunday

*Tsar Nicholas has lost absolutely the affection of the Russian people, and whatever the future may have in store for the Romanovs, Nicholas will never again be safe in the midst of his people.*

**The 1905 Revolution**
Bloody Sunday, together with the defeat of Russia in a war with Japan (1904–5), sparked revolution in Russia. There were strikes and a mutiny in the navy. In order to avoid further chaos, Nicholas II issued the **October Manifesto**, which promised freedom of speech, an end to censorship and a national parliament (***duma***). This revolution was a warning to the tsar about the need for change and reform. However, Nicholas II ignored this warning.

**'Stolypin's necktie'**
After the 1905 Revolution, Nicholas appointed Peter Stolypin as prime minister. Stolypin did introduce certain reforms, especially of agriculture and education. However, those who openly opposed the tsar were dealt with severely. There were more than 3000 executions during Stolypin's time as prime minister – and the gallows became known as 'Stolypin's necktie'.

**The failure of the *dumas***
In the years after 1905 Nicholas ensured that the *duma* he had been forced to create had little power. After the election of the first *duma* in 1906, he declared that he had the power to dissolve it, and to change the rules by which it was elected, whenever he liked. There were four different *dumas* in the years 1906–14. Nicholas had gone against the promises made in his October Manifesto, refusing to share power and continuing to rule like an autocrat. This, in turn, stimulated further opposition.

**Industrial unrest**
As we have seen, Russia's rapid industrial growth had created poor living and working conditions for the industrial workers. This led to a wave of strikes in the years before 1914. One of the most important strikes occurred in 1912 at the Lena goldfields, where troops shot dead more than 200 strikers and injured several hundred. The events at Lena heralded a new wave of strikes in urban areas across Russia and there was a general strike in St Petersburg in July 1914.

## Rasputin

After 1907, Nicholas and his wife, Alexandra, came to rely on the help and guidance of a holy man (starets) named Gregory Rasputin. Rasputin had the ability to control the life-threatening illness (haemophilia) of Alexis, the tsar's son. Alexandra believed that Rasputin had been sent by God and after he saved Alexis' life, she became great friends with him. As Rasputin's influence with Nicholas and Alexandra increased, the press and the *duma* criticised the relationship. This only served to have Nicholas censor articles about Rasputin in the press and this, in turn, increased opposition to the tsar.

Alexandra and Nicholas called Rasputin 'Our Friend' and his position and power at court grew so much that he eventually helped to choose government ministers. (See page 20 for the influence of Rasputin during the war.) There were many aristocrats who disliked the influence of Rasputin, but, equally, there were those who sought his company. Stories about his **hedonistic** lifestyle abounded, such as rumours of orgies, and there were always large numbers of women in his presence.

Rasputin was another piece of ammunition for those who did not like tsarism. These critics saw corruption and incompetence now being added to the list of problems that Russia faced.

**TASKS**

**4** How useful is Source D to a historian studying the importance of Bloody Sunday?
(For guidance on answering this type of question, see pages 59–60.)

**5** Use the information in Source E and your own knowledge to explain why many Russian nobles resented Rasputin.
(For guidance on answering this type of question, see page 40.)

**6** How far does Source F support the view that Rasputin had strong influence over the Royal family?
(For guidance on answering this type of question, see pages 48–49.)

**Source E** From a statement by Rodzianko, an Octobrist politician, March 1916, about the evil influence of Rasputin

*I said to the tsar – 'This cannot continue much longer. No one opens your eyes to the true role which Rasputin is playing. His presence in Your Majesty's Court undermines confidence in your Supreme Power and may have an evil effect ... ' My report did some good – Rasputin was sent away to Tobolsk, but few days later, at the demand of the Empress, this order was cancelled.*

**Source F** One of the many postcards that circulated St Petersburg in 1916 and 1917, showing Rasputin and Alexandra

## Political groups

After the 1905 Revolution, political parties became legal. Before this time, they had to meet in secret and the *Okhrana* had frequently spied on such groups. The main political parties are shown in the boxes below.

**The Social Democratic Party founded in 1901**
The party followed the teachings of **Karl Marx** and believed that the workers (**proletariat**) would one day stage a revolution and remove the tsar. The revolution would lead to the setting up of a Communist state.

In 1903, the party split into two: **Mensheviks** and Bolsheviks. The Mensheviks believed that the party should have a mass membership and were prepared for slow change. The Bolsheviks believed that a small party élite should organise the revolution.

Vladimir Lenin led the Bolsheviks and the Mensheviks were led by Julius Martov and Leon Trotsky.

**The Socialist Revolutionaries (SRs) founded in 1901**
The **Socialist Revolutionaries,** or **SRs** as they were called, believed in a revolution of the peasants and aimed to get rid of the tsar. They wanted to share all land among the peasants, so that it could be farmed in small peasant communities.

There was a mixture of beliefs within the party – some wanted to use terror to achieve their aims and others were prepared to use constitutional methods. Terrorist activity by SR members led to the deaths of thousands of government officials in the years before 1917.

Alexander Kerensky eventually led the SRs.

**The Constitutional Democratic Party (Cadets) founded in 1905**
As Russia developed a middle class, the demand grew for a democratic style of government. The **Cadets** wanted to have a constitutional monarch and an elected parliament – as in Britain – though some were prepared to set up a republic.

The Cadets were led by Paul Milyukov.

**The Octobrists founded in October 1905**
This party was set up after the tsar issued his October Manifesto. Its followers believed that the tsar would carry out his manifesto promises of limited reform. The **Octobrists**' main area of support came from the middle classes.

The Octobrists were led by Alexander Guchkov.

### TASKS

**7** Which of the political parties might Tsar Nicholas II have feared the most? Explain your answer.

**8** Working in pairs, devise a catchy slogan for each of the four parties.

**9** Copy the table below and then fill in the columns, explaining how each issue contributed to the growing opposition to the tsar in the years before 1917.

| Political issues | Economic issues | Social issues |
|---|---|---|
| | | |

# What was Russia's experience in the First World War?

Russia entered the First World War in 1914 with great expectations of success. Many believed that the sheer size of the Russian armies, known as the Russian steamroller, would be too strong for both Germany and Austria-Hungary. However, by the end of 1916, Russia had suffered defeat after defeat (see timeline opposite) and there was growing discontent with the tsar and his government.

The map below and the timeline on page 17 show the key events in the war from 1914 to 1916.

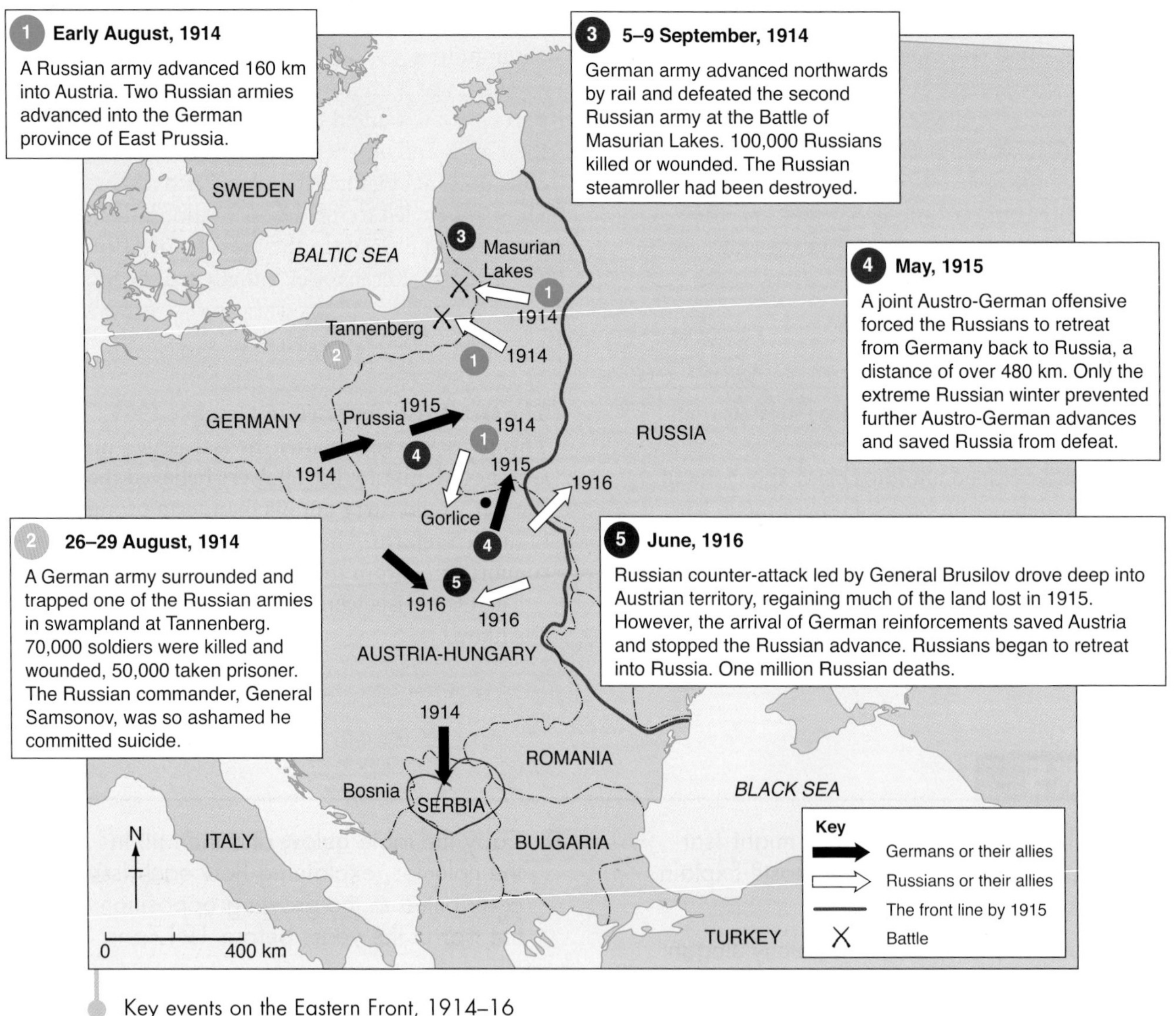


Key events on the Eastern Front, 1914–16

| DATE | EVENT |
|---|---|
| **1914** | |
| August | Russians advanced into Austria and Germany |
| 26–9 August | Battle of Tannenberg |
| 5–9 September | Battle of Masurian Lakes |
| | *By the end of 1914 Russia had over 1 million casualties* |
| **1915** | |
| May | Austro-German offensive |
| August | Nicholas took command of the Russian armies |
| | *By the end of 1915 Germany and Austria-Hungary had control of 13 per cent of the Russian population including 16 million people* |
| **1916** | |
| June | Brusilov offensive |
| Winter | All gains from Brusilov offensive lost |

Timeline of events on the Eastern Front, 1914–16

**Source A** An extract from the diary of Meriel Buchanan, the daughter of the British Ambassador to Russia. She describes the reaction to Russian entry into the First World War, 5 August 1914

*The processions in the streets were carrying the Emperor's portrait with the bands playing the national anthem. Women and girls flocked to work in the hospitals. Everywhere there is enthusiasm for the war. People are convinced that we are fighting in a just and holy war for the freedom and betterment of the world. We dream of triumph and victory. The war will be over by Christmas.*

**Source B** The German general, von Moltke, describes the slaughter at Tannenberg

*The sight of thousands of Russians driven into huge lakes and swamps was ghastly. The shrieks and cries of the dying men I will never forget. So fearful was the sight of these thousands of men with their guns, horses and ammunition, struggling in the water that, to shorten their agony, they turned the machine-guns on them. But even in spite of that, there was movement seen among them for a week after.*

## TASKS

1. What does Source A show you about reactions in Russia to the outbreak of war?
2. How useful is Source B to a historian studying the Battle of Tannenberg? (For guidance on answering this type of question, see pages 59–60.)

# Why did Russia suffer so many defeats and what were the effects?

## Reasons for defeat

The main reasons for Russian defeats in the war were poor leadership and lack of infrastructure and supplies. These reasons are explored in the concept map below.

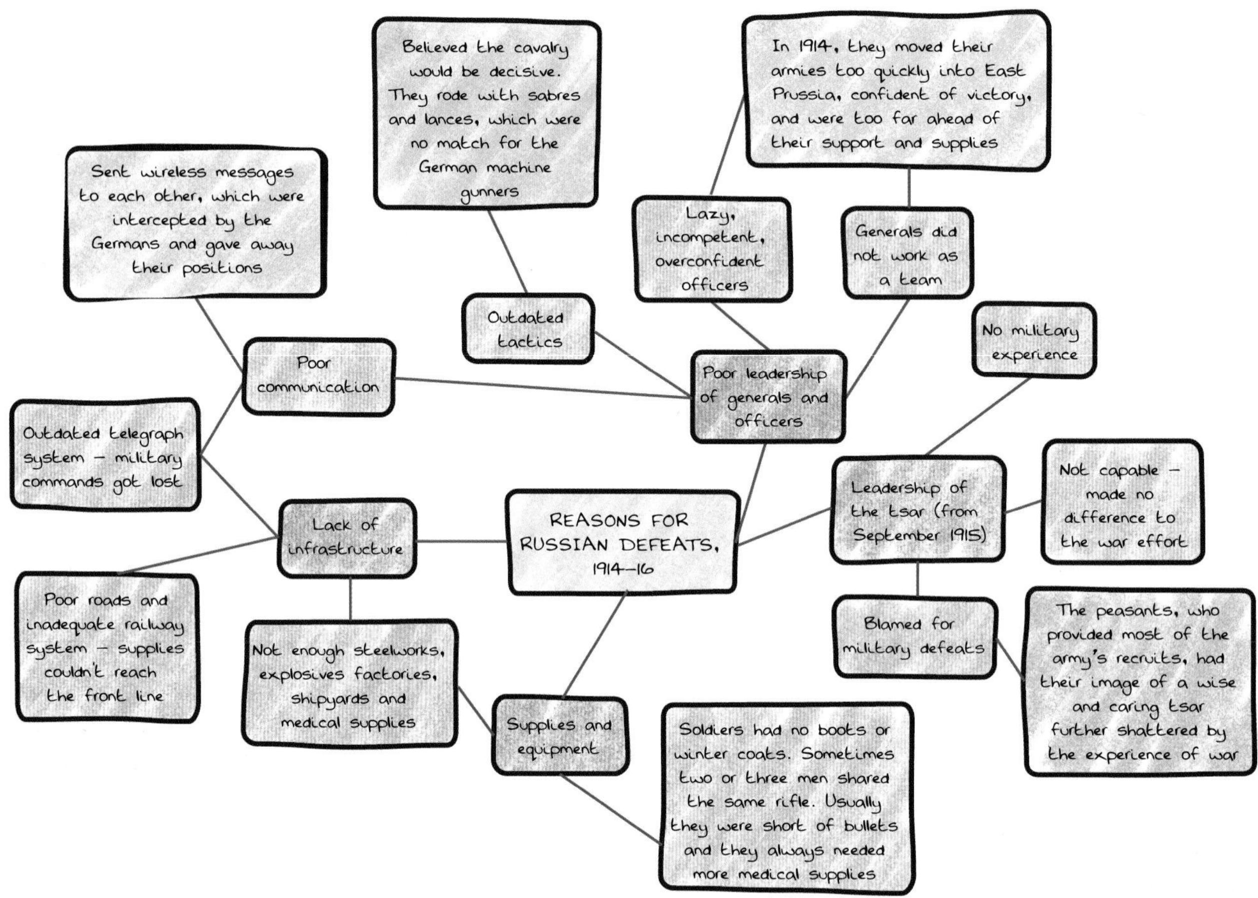


**Source A** From a letter written by the tsar to his wife in July 1916

*Without metal the mills cannot supply a sufficient number of bullets and bombs. The same is true as regards the railways. The Minister of Transportation assures me that the railways are working better this year than last, but nevertheless every one complains that they are not doing as well as they might.*

**Source B** From a letter written by General Beliaev at the front to the *duma*, 1916

*In recent battles, a third of the men had no rifles. The poor devils had to wait patiently until their comrades fell before their eyes and they could pick up weapons. The army is drowning in its own blood.*

## Military effects of the defeats

Enthusiasm for the war soon waned. Casualties, frequent defeats and poor equipment made the morale of the soldiers low. They soon lost respect for their officers who seemed unfeeling and ineffective. Many soldiers died without weapons or ammunition, and some did not even have boots to wear in the bitterly cold weather. This discontent spread to the people of Russia. News of high casualties caused alarm in different parts of the Russian Empire.

**Source C** From an official report by the Chairman of the Military Commission of the *duma*, 1916

*As early as the beginning of the second year of the war, desertions of soldiers at the front and on their way to the front became commonplace, and the average number of deserters reached 25 per cent. I happen to know of three cases when the train was stopped because there were no passengers on it; all, with the exception of the officer in command, had run away.*

**Source D** A photograph showing Russian deserters, including officers, in December 1916

## TASKS

1. Examine the concept map opposite, which shows the key reasons for Russia's defeats.
   - Explain how the different reasons are linked.
   - Rank the reasons in order of importance in the defeat of Russia. Explain the reasons for your ordering.
2. Explain why Russia suffered many defeats in the years 1914–16.
   (For guidance on answering this type of question, see page 90.)
3. You are an adviser to Nicholas II who has been sent to the Eastern Front to investigate the situation in September 1915. Write a memorandum to the tsar explaining the problems at the front and what needs to be done. Use Sources A and B and the concept map to help you.
4. How useful is Source C to a historian studying the effects of the war on the Russian soldiers?
   (For guidance on answering this type of question, see pages 59–60.)
5. How far does Source D support the evidence of Source C about the behaviour of some Russian soldiers?
6. Study Source D. This photograph was probably taken by opponents of the tsar and the war. Devise a caption that they could have used with this photograph.

## Economic effects of the defeats

The war had a devastating effect on the Russian economy. Inflation increased at a tremendous rate. Less food was produced because of the shortage of labour and horses. As more peasants were called up to the armed forces, there were fewer men left to work on the land. Indeed, 14 million men were called up to serve in the army between 1914 and 1917. The demand for horses at the front also made it harder for peasants to cultivate their land. This, in turn, encouraged higher food prices.

Industry, too, was hit by the shortage of workers and by the lack of fuel and essential supplies. Russia did not have a transport system that could cope with the increased demands of war, as well as providing industry with the necessary raw materials. Consumer goods such as boots and cloth became scarce and expensive. There were shortages of essential coal, iron and steel. Many factories closed, making their workers unemployed.

The economic problems brought misery for many Russians. Because of the shortages, the prices were rising continually, but wages were hardly going up at all. To make matters worse, workers were asked to work longer hours. The closure of factories led to unemployment and even greater poverty. All these hardships were, in turn, worsened by the increasing fuel and food shortages. Even when fuel and food were available they frequently failed to reach the people in the towns and cities, as a result of Russia's inadequate transport system and the incompetence of the government.

**Source E** From an official police report, December 1916

*The industrial proletariat of the capital is on the verge of despair. The smallest outbreak will lead to uncontrollable riots. Even if we assume that wages have increased by 100 per cent, the cost of living has risen by 300 per cent. The impossibility of obtaining food, the time wasted in queues outside shops, the increasing death rate due to inadequate diet and the cold and dampness as a result of the lack of coal and firewood – all these conditions have created such a situation that the mass of industrial workers are quite ready to let themselves go to the wildest excesses of a hunger riot.*

## TASKS

**7** Use the information in Source E and your own knowledge to explain why Russia was facing severe problems by the end of 1916. (For guidance on answering this type of question, see page 40.)

**8** Use Sources E and F to explain why life was getting harder for Russian workers by 1917.

## Mass discontent

By the beginning of 1917, Russia was close to defeat on the Eastern Front and there was mass discontent in the armed forces and among the Russian people. To make matters worse, Petrograd (the name St Petersburg was changed to Petrograd during the war because Russians hated anything which sounded German) experienced the worst winter in living memory with temperatures falling below –30°C, at a time when there were severe food and fuel shortages.

**Source F** Wages and prices in Petrograd, 1914 and 1917

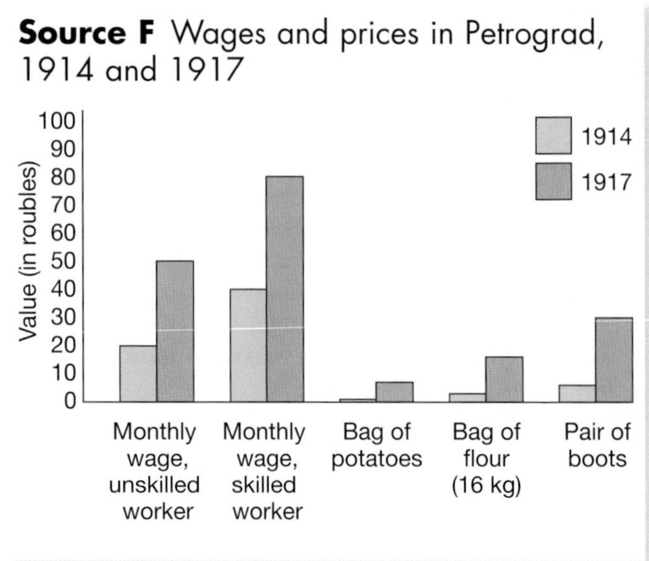


## Political effects of the defeats

At first, the war seemed to improve the government of Russia as it encouraged the tsar to work with the *duma*, but ultimately the war seriously weakened the position of the tsar.

Nicholas' decision to take over command of the war and move to the front in August 1915 was a serious political mistake, and he was now blamed for the military defeats. It also meant that he left the running of the country in the hands of his wife, Alexandra, the tsarina. She refused to take advice from middle-class members of the *duma* and they became increasingly frustrated, convinced that they could do a better job.

During the war, the Russian people grew to hate anything German. Alexandra was German and there were rumours that she was a German spy trying to sabotage the Russian war effort.

Rasputin was the only person Alexandra was prepared to listen to and there were rumours that they were having an affair. Indeed, he seemed to be in charge of the government. The tsarina frequently dismissed any capable ministers from the *duma* on Rasputin's advice and replaced them with his own friends, who were totally incompetent. There were so many changes of ministers that nobody was organising food, fuel and other supplies to the cities properly. The railway system fell into chaos and trainloads of food were left rotting.

As news from the war got worse and the situation in the cities got more desperate, support for the tsar and his wife began to decrease among the middle and upper classes. They blamed the tsar for leaving the country under the control of a German woman influenced by a mad monk.

**Source G** From a letter to a friend written by Lenin, the leader of the Bolsheviks, in December 1916

*A total absence of patriotic feeling can be seen in the mood of the working masses. The high cost of living, exploitation, and the barbaric policy of the government has proved to the masses the true nature of the war. There is an increase in strikes throughout the country. Prices have gone up five to ten times compared to last year. Clothing and footwear are becoming unobtainable and you no longer talk about meat.*

## The death of Rasputin

Members of the royal family begged Alexandra to dismiss Rasputin. When she refused, some, led by Prince Yusupov, in desperation, decided to assassinate him. One evening in December 1916, Rasputin was invited to Yusupov's mansion for a social evening. During the course of the evening he ate cakes laced with enough cyanide to kill several men. He collapsed but then stood up and ran into the courtyard. There he was shot twice. His hands were bound behind him and his body thrown into the icy river where he drowned.

Yet the death of Rasputin did not end the discontent, and support for Tsar Nicholas continued to diminish. By the end of 1916, Russia was in a chaotic state. 1917 brought disaster and, in February, Nicholas II abdicated and the monarchy came to an end.

## TASKS

**9** How far does Source F support the view that inflation was a serious problem in Russia by 1917? (For guidance on answering this type of question, see pages 48–49.)

**10** How useful is Source G to a historian studying conditions in Russia by the end of 1916? (For guidance on answering this type of question, see pages 59–60.)

**11** Look at the circles below. This is known as a Venn diagram. They are used to show how factors can overlap with each other – how one factor can influence another.

- Sketch your own Venn diagram like the one below.
- Use your diagram to show the overlap between the military, political, economic/social effects. One example has been done for you, showing the leadership of Rasputin and the tsarina.

**12** Use the internet and other resources to research the exact details surrounding the death of Rasputin. Write up your findings into a report using the headline 'The murder of Rasputin'.

**13** How important was Rasputin in increasing opposition to the rule of the tsar?
(For guidance on answering this type of question, see page 113.)

# Examination guidance

This section provides guidance on how to answer the comprehension of a visual source question. It is worth 2 marks.

What does Source A show you about conditions in Russia in early 1917? (2 marks)

**Source A** This photograph shows Russians queuing for bread in Petrograd in early 1917

## Tips on how to answer

This is an inference question involving the comprehension of a visual source.

- You are being asked to **look into the picture** and **pick out** relevant details.
- You must also **make use of the caption attached to the source** which is intended to provide you with additional information.
- You must **only comment on what you can see** in the picture and the caption attached to the source. **Do not** bring in additional factual knowledge as this will not score you marks.
- To obtain maximum marks you will need to **pick out at least two relevant points** which are well developed and supported.

### Response by candidate

*Source A shows that conditions were harsh and there were food shortages in Russia in early 1917. Large numbers of people in Petrograd had to queue up in the rain for basic food supplies such as bread.*

### Examiner's comment

The candidate has made a number of valid observations based upon the source and its caption. There is a clear understanding that conditions in 1917 were very harsh and food was in short supply. People had to queue for even basic supplies. This is a developed answer worthy of the maximum of 2 marks.

# What were the main developments during the Bolshevik seizure of power?

By the beginning of January 1917, the position in Russia had become chaotic. Defeats in the war, food shortages and lack of social and political reform meant that support for the tsar had been severely eroded. At the end of February, Nicholas abdicated and a Provisional Government was set up to run Russia until elections could be held. After the elections, a permanent government would be established. The Provisional Government had some successes initially but, almost from the beginning, it had to share power with the Petrograd Soviet. This power sharing was called **Dual Power** or Dual Authority and it reduced the effectiveness of the Provisional Government. By the autumn of 1917, there was tremendous dissatisfaction with the Provisional Government and the Bolsheviks felt they could challenge for power. They seized power in October.

This chapter answers the following questions:

- Why was there a revolution in Russia in February 1917?
- Why did rivalry emerge between the Provisional Government and the Petrograd Soviet?
- How did the Bolsheviks seize power in October 1917?
- What were the main events of the Bolshevik Revolution?
- Why were the Bolsheviks successful in October 1917?

**Source A** From a letter written in February 1917 by a 14-year-old boy describing the situation in Petrograd

*Terrible things are happening in Petrograd. It has become a real battlefield. Five regiments of the army have joined the revolt. Gunfire never ceases in our part of the city. The officers cannot go into the streets, because the crowd disarms them and even kills them ... Worst of all, the soldiers have got hold of vodka and are drunk.*

**TASK**

What does Source A show you about the situation in Petrograd in February 1917?

**Examination guidance**

Throughout this chapter you will be given the opportunity to practise different exam-style questions and detailed guidance on how to answer a source comprehension question which is linked to the recall of your own knowledge. This is worth 4 marks.

# Why was there a revolution in Russia in February 1917?

**Source A** From a letter written by Grand Duke Michael to the tsar in January 1917. He was describing the problems facing Russia at that time

*The unrest continues to grow. Those who defend the idea that Russia cannot exist without a tsar are losing the ground under their feet, since the facts of disorganisation and lawlessness are obvious. A situation like this cannot last long. It is impossible to rule the country without paying attention to the voice of the people and without meeting their needs.*

**Source B** From an *Okhrana* report in January 1917 describing the mood in Petrograd

*The proletariat of the capital is on the verge of despair. Time wasted in queues hoping for food to arrive, the increasing death rate due to inadequate diet, cold and dampness as a result of lack of coal and firewood, have created a situation whereby the mass of industrial workers are quite ready to let themselves go to the wildest excesses of a hunger riot ... the masses assume an openly hostile attitude towards the government and protest against the continuation of the war.*

As you have learned in Chapter 1, the First World War placed a tremendous strain on Russia and, by early 1917, the country was on the verge of collapse. It had been hoped that the death of Rasputin in December 1916 would help to bring some stability to the running of the country – it did not. The winter weather was especially severe in December and January and this meant that food supplies to cities and towns were affected. Prices continued to rise and rationing only led to further discontent. In Petrograd, there were strikes and people began to demand food.

| The events in Petrograd, 14–28 February 1917 | |
|---|---|
| *14 February* | The President of the *duma*, Rodzianko, informed Nicholas that he could no longer rely on his closest supporters in Petrograd. |
| *18 February* | A strike at the Putilov engineering works began. The workers wanted higher wages as a result of inflation. |
| *23 February* | International Women's Day organised by socialist groups – this meant that large numbers of women joined about 100,000 strikers and demonstrators on the streets of Petrograd. Many women chanted simple slogans such as 'Down with hunger!' and 'Bread for the workers!' |
| *24 February* | Approximately 200,000 workers on strike. |
| *25 February* | Strikes all over the city with about 300,000 demonstrators on the streets. No newspapers printed and no public transport. The police began to show sympathy for the demonstrators. |
| *26 February* | Nicholas instructed the army to restore order but some of the Petrograd garrison had deserted. Some shots were fired on the demonstrators. There were no printers to produce the tsar's proclamations. |
| *27 February* | Buildings, shops and restaurants were looted. Most of the Petrograd garrison mutinied. Nicholas ordered the *duma* to dissolve. It did so but twelve members refused and set up a 'Provisional Committee'. Alexander Kerensky, a Socialist Revolutionary, demanded that Nicholas **abdicate**.<br>First meeting of the re-formed Petrograd Soviet of Soldiers' Sailors' and Workers' Deputies.<br>The Provisional Committee and the Petrograd Soviet were now running the country. |
| *28 February* | The Petrograd Soviet issued the newspaper *Izvestiya* (*The News*) and declared its intention to remove the old system of government. |

Strikes became an everyday occurrence in Petrograd in early 1917 and this resulted in huge numbers of people on the streets. The situation worsened when the soldiers garrisoned in Petrograd mutinied and began to take sides with the demonstrators. For Nicholas, this was disastrous – a loyal army had saved him in the 1905 Revolution – now his final pillar of support started to crumble.

Nicholas' presence at the front meant that he did not always know exactly what was happening in Petrograd. He would not accept advice from the *duma* which he had recalled in 1915. Events began to spiral out of control in February 1917.

**Source C** International Women's Day demonstration, Petrograd, 1917. The main banner calls for women to establish an assembly and the one at the front says 'Freedom for the citizens of Russia'

## TASKS

1. How far does Source A support the view that Russia was on the verge of revolution at the beginning of 1917? (For guidance on answering this type of question, see pages 48–49.)
2. How useful is Source B to a historian studying the effects of the war on the Russian people? (For guidance on answering this type of question, see pages 59–60.)
3. What does Source C show you about the extent of unrest in Petrograd in 1917? (For guidance on answering this type of question, see page 22.)
4. Study Source D, Rodzianko's two telegrams to Tsar Nicholas. Can you suggest reasons why Nicholas failed to respond to the growing problems in Petrograd?

**Source D** Telegrams from Rodzianko, president of the *duma*, to Tsar Nicholas II on 26 and 27 February 1917

**Telegram of 26 February 1917**

The situation is serious. The capital is in a state of anarchy. The government is paralysed; the transportation system has broken down; the supply systems for food and fuel are completely disorganised. General discontent is on the increase. There is disorderly shooting in the streets; some of the troops are firing at each other. It is necessary that some person enjoying the confidence of the country be entrusted immediately with the formation of a new government. There can be no delay. Any hesitation is fatal.

**Telegram of 27 February 1917**

The situation is growing worse. Measures must be taken, immediately, for tomorrow will already be too late. The final hour has struck when the fate of the country and the dynasty is being decided. The government is powerless to stop the disorders. The troops of the garrison cannot be relied upon. The reserve battalions of the guard regiments are in the grips of rebellion, their officers are being killed. Having joined the mobs and revolt of the people, they are marching on the offices of the Ministry of the Interior and the Imperial Duma. Your majesty, do not delay. Should the agitation reach the army, Germany will triumph and the destruction of Russia along with the dynasty is inevitable.

## The abdication of Tsar Nicholas II

| The events in Petrograd, 1–3 March 1917 | |
|---|---|
| *1 March* | The Petrograd Soviet issued Soviet Order Number One which took away all authority from army officers and transferred it to the elected representatives of the soldiers. |
| *2 March* | Nicholas decided to return to Petrograd and was met at Pskov, where his leading generals advised that his presence there would do no good. They advised him to abdicate.<br>Nicholas abdicated and refused to nominate his son Alexei as his successor because of his haemophilia. Nicholas' brother, the Grand Duke Michael, was then proposed as the new tsar, but he declined. |
| *3 March* | The Provisional Committee renamed itself the Provisional Government and became responsible for running the country. |

The Romanov dynasty had reached the point where it ended itself. The abdication of Nicholas and the emergence of the Provisional Government out of the *duma* is called the February Revolution. The abdication took place in a railway carriage 320 km from Petrograd (see Source E).

**Source E** The abdication of Nicholas II, March 1917. Nicholas is seated

**Source F** From *History of the Russian Revolution* by Leon Trotsky. Trotsky was one of the leaders of the Bolsheviks in the October Revolution

*It would be no exaggeration to say that Petrograd achieved the February Revolution. The rest of the country adhered to it. There was no struggle anywhere except in Petrograd. Nowhere in the country were there any groups of the population, any parties, institutions or military units ready to put up a fight for the old regime. Neither at the front nor at the rear was there a brigade or regiment prepared to do battle for Nicholas II.*

### TASKS

**5** What does Source E show you about the end of the Romanov dynasty in Russia? (For guidance on answering this type of question, see page 22.)

**6** Some historians have said that 27 February was the most important day in the Revolution. Why do you think this is the case? Explain your reasons.

**7** Study Source F. Explain why Trotsky thought Petrograd had been crucial in the February Revolution.

**8** Reread pages 24–25. What were the causes of the February Revolution? Draw a table and place the causes of the revolution under the following headings, then number them in what you think is their order of importance.

| Impact of the war | Social problems | Mistakes of the tsar | Economic problems | Political problems |
|---|---|---|---|---|
| | | | | |

**9** Reread Chapter 1 and pages 23–26. Make a list of the long-term causes of the revolution and then a list of the short-term causes.

# Why did rivalry emerge between the Provisional Government and the Petrograd Soviet?

The end of tsarism was unplanned and took people by surprise. The Provisional Government was set up on 3 March 1917 and it promised to bring reforms to Russia. There would also be elections for a new **Constituent Assembly** (parliament) as soon as possible. The Provisional Government consisted of a cabinet of ministers. The Prime Minister was Prince Lvov, a wealthy aristocratic landowner, and other leading figures included:

- Milyukov – Foreign Minister and leader of the Cadets
- Guchkov – War Minister and leader of the Octobrists
- Kerensky – Minister of Justice and Socialist Revolutionary.

The remaining ministers were chosen from the Octobrist and Cadet parties. Thus, the new government was composed of middle-class politicians who wanted to draw up a constitution and establish a democratic government. Initially, it was supported by the Bolsheviks, who believed that the working classes could become better organised under such a government. Then, in the future, the workers would be able to seize power from the middle classes.

## Problems

The Provisional Government faced a number of problems as soon as it was formed:

- it was not a truly elected body and did not represent the people of Russia
- there were further defeats in the war
- soldiers continued to desert
- peasants were looting the property of the landlords
- soldiers and workers were setting up soviets in towns and cities across Russia
- people wanted an end to food shortages
- some of the national minorities in Russia, for example, Poles and Finns, were hoping that there might even be a chance of independence in the near future.

Perhaps the most serious issue facing the Provisional Government was the existence of the Petrograd Soviet of Workers' and Soldiers' Deputies. The existence of the Provisional Government and the Petrograd Soviet meant that there were two bodies running Russia. This became known as the Dual Power.

## The Petrograd Soviet

By early March, the Soviet had about 3000 elected members and contained many revolutionaries, especially Socialist Revolutionaries and Mensheviks (see page 15). These members of the Soviet were happy to work with the Provisional Government because it was fulfilling the ideas of Karl Marx (see diagram below). They believed that the Provisional Government was the **bourgeois** phase before the workers' revolution and, when the government failed, the Soviet would take over Russia on behalf of the workers.

**History was shaped by the struggles between different social classes...**

As society changed from *feudalism* to *capitalism*, there were struggles between the aristocracy and the middle classes. The middle classes were able to take power from the aristocrats and began to exploit the workers in the new industrial world.

The workers (proletariat) would eventually rebel against their exploitation and set up a socialist state.

Eventually, the ideal state would be created – communism, where everyone was equal and people worked for the good of the commune or state.

**...Marx's interpretation of history meant that a successful proletarian revolution could only occur where there was an industrial society.**

The theory of Marxism

## The Dual Power

Both the Provisional Government and the Petrograd Soviet met in the same building in Petrograd, the Tauride Palace. Initially, they worked together, but as the months wore on, the issues of fighting the war and redistributing land gradually created a split between the two bodies.

The Provisional Government was described as 'the authority without power' and the Petrograd Soviet was described as 'the power without authority'.

## Soviet Order Number One

The Petrograd Soviet issued Soviet Order Number One (see Source A) and it was this which took away much of the authority of the new government. The Soviet only wished to continue the war until the German army was pushed out of Russia, and disagreed with the Provisional Government which was prepared to fight on with Britain and France until Germany surrendered. The Soviet also wanted to redistribute land among the peasants but the Provisional Government was unwilling to do this because many of its supporters were landowners.

**Source A** Soviet Order Number One, 14 March 1917

*The Soviet of Workers' and Soldiers' Deputies has resolved:*

- *In all its political actions, troop units are subordinate to the Soviet.*
- *All types of arms must be kept under the control of the company and battalion committees and in no case turned over to officers, even at their demand.*
- *The orders of the state duma shall be executed only in such cases as do not conflict with the orders of the Soviet of Workers' and Soldiers' Deputies.*

**Source B** A letter from the Russian Minister for War in the Provisional Government to General Alekseev, 22 March 1917

*The Provisional Government possesses no real power and its orders are only executed in so far as it is permitted by the Soviet of Workers' and Soldiers' Deputies, which holds in its hands the most important elements of actual power, such as troops, railroads, postal and telegraph service ... .*

## The June offensive

Despite Soviet Order Number One, the Provisional Government decided to continue the war because it was concerned at the heavy demands Germany would make if Russia sought peace. Alexander Kerensky, the Minister for War, visited the troops and persuaded them to support a new offensive. Surprisingly, the Petrograd Soviet agreed and supported Kerensky's June offensive in the hope that it would drive the German forces out of Russia. There were even some Bolsheviks – Stalin and Kamenev – who felt that the war should not be stopped.

However, the decision to continue the war was fatal for the Provisional Government because further defeats served only to increase its unpopularity. Kerensky's June offensive was a failure and resulted in more than 60,000 deaths and yet more desertions. When soldiers returned home they took part in seizing land from the nobility – thus worsening the chaos across Russia.

To add to the misery of the Provisional Government, Germany sent exiled revolutionaries back to Russia in the hope that they would stir up rebellion. Among these was Lenin, the Bolshevik leader, who had arrived in Petrograd in April 1917. Lenin called for the overthrow of the Provisional Government.

### TASKS

**1** Look at all the problems that faced the Provisional Government (pages 27–28). Copy the table below, placing the problems in the appropriate column, and number them in what you think is their order of importance.

| Political problems | Economic problems | Military problems |
|---|---|---|
| | | |
| | | |
| | | |
| | | |
| | | |

**2** Explain why Soviet Order Number One in Source A was so important in undermining the Provisional Government.

## The Provisional Government's reforms

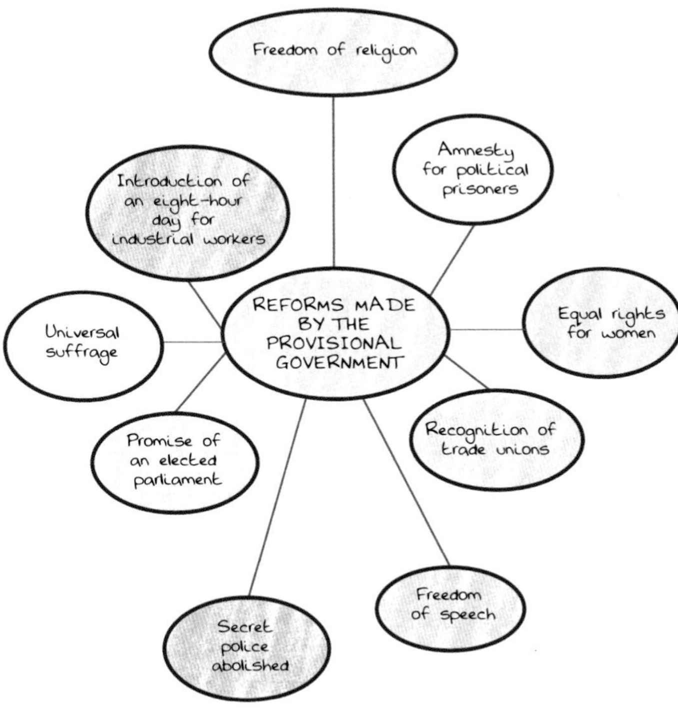


Despite its many problems, the Provisional Government did introduce some reforms during the early weeks of its ministry (see diagram above).

Many of the reforms were pushed through by Alexander Kerensky, the Minister of Justice. Each reform tried to address problems which either had not been solved after the 1905 Revolution, or had been created by the tsar and his ministers in an effort to keep a tight control over the Russian people.

The reforms were quite wide-ranging and it was hoped that the workers and the middle classes would be satisfied by them. Kerensky won great personal support with his powerful speeches. Being a member of both the Provisional Government and the Petrograd Soviet placed him in a unique position and he could readily see what each body was seeking.

**Biography** Alexander Kerensky 1881–1970

1881 Born in Simbirsk

1899 Attended St Petersburg University. Gained law degree

1905 Jailed on suspicion of belonging to a militant group. Afterwards he worked as a defence lawyer in a number of political trials of revolutionaries

1912 Elected to the Fourth *Duma*, 1912 as a member of the Trudoviks, a moderate labour party

1917 As Minister of Justice Kerensky was responsible for the introduction of numerous basic civil liberties, including freedom of speech, press, assembly and religion, universal suffrage and equal rights for women
Became a Member of the Provisional Committee of the state *duma* in February.
Elected vice-chairman of the Petrograd Soviet. He was seen as the link between the two bodies
Appointed Minister of War in the Provisional Government in May
Appointed Prime Minister in the Provisional Government in July
Appointed Chief of armed forces in August
Fled to France in November

1970 Died in New York in exile

## TASKS

**3** Use the information in Source B and your own knowledge to explain why the Petrograd Soviet was in a powerful position in March 1917. (For guidance on answering this type of question, see page 40.)

**4** Explain what is meant by the phrases 'the authority without power' and 'the power without authority'.

**5** Look at the diagram of the Provisional Government's reforms. Choose the three most important and explain each choice.

**6** Describe the political career of Alexander Kerensky. (For guidance on answering this type of question, see page 79.)

## The return of Lenin

When war broke out in 1914, Lenin was in Austria. He was arrested, but allowed to travel to Zürich in neutral Switzerland. He was utterly opposed to the war, but found that there were many Bolsheviks who supported it. After the February Revolution, Lenin was desperate to return to Russia. He was keen that his supporters at home put forward the message that the Bolsheviks wanted peace and an end to the chaos in Russia. The Germans decided to help Lenin return from exile in Switzerland, in the hope that he would overthrow the new government in Russia. The Germans thought that if Russia pulled out of the war, then more troops could be moved to the **Western Front** to fight Britain and France.

Lenin was put in a sealed train and sent across Germany and Sweden. He arrived in Petrograd's Finland rail station on 3 April 1917. The price to pay for this method of arrival was the accusation that he was a German spy, in the pay of the enemy. Lenin was unconcerned. He had returned and, moreover, the money from the Germans would help to finance his revolution.

## The April Theses

Lenin made it clear to his followers that he would not support the Provisional Government. He wanted a workers' revolution and his plans were set out the day after his return, in what became known as the April Theses.

**The April Theses**

i The war with Germany had to end.
ii Power had to pass from the middle classes to the working classes.
iii All land had to be given to the peasants.
iv The police, army and bureaucracy should be abolished.
v The capitalist system had to be overthrown by the workers – banks, factories and transport should be nationalised.
vi The Bolsheviks should take control of the soviets in order to achieve their aims. The slogan 'All power to the soviets' became the watchword.

**Source C** A scene by Brodski painted in 1929, which shows Lenin addressing the workers of the Putilov factory in May 1917

The Bolsheviks began to grow in popularity and, by June 1917, there were more than 40 newspapers that spread Lenin's views and ideas across Russia. The Bolsheviks even had their own armed force – the **Red Guard**. By July, there were about 10,000 armed workers in Petrograd itself. The Red Guard was increasing in size daily with the arrival of army deserters.

**Source D** Membership of the Bolshevik Party, 1917

- *February*: 24,000
- *April*: 100,000
- *October*: 340,000 (60,000 in Petrograd)

## The July Days

Despite attempted reforms, by July, the Provisional Government was still experiencing problems. The war was not going well and the growing power of the soviets across Russia and strength of opposition were key concerns. The sharing of Dual Power was coming under increasing strain. The Austrian Front was disintegrating and this caused many soldiers to flood back to Russia. For three days, there was chaos in Petrograd when the soldiers and some Bolsheviks tried to overthrow the Provisional Government. These are known as the July Days. Lenin felt that the Bolsheviks had grown sufficiently to challenge the Provisional Government, which had done little to put right the grievances of the people.

The riots and disorder were only calmed when Kerensky, the Minister of War, was able to move loyal troops to quash the rebels. About 400 people were killed and injured during the July Days and Kerensky claimed that the Bolsheviks, who had been involved in the trouble, were in the pay of Germany. When Lenin fled the country and other leading Bolsheviks were arrested or went into hiding, it appeared as if the Bolsheviks' chance to seize power had gone and that the party was in decline.

**Source E** Demonstrators in Petrograd being fired upon by police during the July Days, 1917

### TASKS

**7** What does Source C show you about the influence of Lenin in 1917? (For guidance on answering this type of question, see page 22.)

**8** How far does Source D support the view that Lenin played an important part in attracting support for the Bolsheviks in the summer of 1917? (For guidance on answering this type of question, see pages 48–49.)

**9** Construct a table like the one below and explain why each group would support or oppose the April Theses.

| | Support | Oppose |
|---|---|---|
| Workers | | |
| Middle classes | | |
| Peasants | | |
| Soldiers | | |

**10** How far does Source E support the view that the Provisional Government had difficulty in maintaining law and order during July 1917? (For guidance on answering this type of question, see pages 48–49.)

## Consequences of the July Days

- A new government was set up with Kerensky as Prime Minister. He accused the Bolsheviks of being German spies, because he knew that Lenin's return to Russia had been financed by Germany. Moreover, much of the Bolsheviks' revolutionary activity since April had been backed by German money.
- Kerensky cemented his position as the most powerful politician in Russia. His reforms as Minister of Justice and his forceful speeches kept the support of many workers and peasants.
- The Bolsheviks were denounced as traitors – their newspaper, ***Pravda*** (*Truth*), was closed down, Lenin fled the country and Kamenev was arrested.

**Source F** A cartoon from *Petrogradskaia Gazeta*, 7 July 1917, a pro-government newspaper. The caption at the top reads 'A high post for the leaders of the rebellion'. The caption below reads 'Lenin wants a high post? ... Well? A position is ready for him!!!'

However, the Bolsheviks were not finished. Lenin directed them from Finland and they were able to continue to function and maintain their high profile. Lenin altered his views about the peasants and their role in any revolution. He accepted the land seizures and encouraged even more, thus winning support in the countryside. The slogan 'land to the peasants' was taken up by the Bolsheviks.

Furthermore, Lenin knew that the Russian army could be swayed towards the Bolshevik anti-war policy – the majority of soldiers were really 'peasants in uniform'. The new Bolshevik slogan of 'Peace, Land and Bread' began to attract more and more followers during these critical times. Soviets had sprung up across Russia and had taken control of local areas and so Lenin began to use the simple slogan – 'All power to the soviets'. Many Bolsheviks came to realise that if they controlled the soviets across Russia then they would come closer to securing power in the country.

## The Kornilov Revolt

After the July Days, Alexander Kerensky had been appointed the new Prime Minister. It seemed as if the Provisional Government was in control – but it was not. This was shown in the Kornilov Revolt. In September 1917, General Kornilov, the Supreme Commander-in-Chief of the armed forces, threatened to seize power in Petrograd. Kornilov did not agree with the Petrograd Soviet's wish to end the war and he sought to set up a military **dictatorship**.

As Kornilov and his forces approached Petrograd, Kerensky allowed the Bolshevik Red Guards to arm and was happy to see the Bolsheviks persuade many of Kornilov's troops to desert. Railway workers prevented Kornilov's troops from approaching Petrograd and printers stopped publication of newspapers that supported the ***coup d'état***. The attempted coup failed and Kornilov was arrested. With the arrest of Kornilov, the Army High Command had lost its Commander-in-Chief and morale sank even lower. Moreover, officers continued to be murdered and desertions reached an even higher level. The army was no longer in a position to set up a military dictatorship.

Kerensky now looked rather weak (see Source G) because it was clear that the Bolsheviks had saved the Provisional Government. The Bolsheviks, who had secured control of the Petrograd and Moscow Soviets, were in the ascendancy. As a result of Kornilov's failure, Lenin could show that the Bolsheviks had helped to save Petrograd. He saw that support for the Bolsheviks was growing not only in Petrograd but in other urban areas. Therefore, Lenin began to make plans for his return from exile in Finland to Petrograd and also for the Bolshevik seizure of power.

For Lenin and Trotsky, the most important feature of the Kornilov Revolt was the arming of the Bolshevik Red Guard. This would be vital when they decided to seize power.

**Source G** From *The Russian Revolution* by D. Footman, a British historian, 1962

*After the Kornilov Revolt, Kerensky and his cabinet were still in power. But there had been a striking change in the mood throughout the country. The Bolsheviks could now claim to have been the leaders in the 'victory over the counter-revolution' and their power and influence increased rapidly.*

## The end of the Provisional Government

All the problems that the Provisional Government had faced in February had not gone away and by October it retained little authority. Lenin's promises of 'Peace, Land and Bread', were proving more attractive than the seeming inaction of Kerensky. It is ironic that when Kerensky did act – setting the date of the elections for the Constituent Assembly – it pushed Lenin to decide on a takeover. Lenin said the Provisional Government was 'ripe for the plucking'.

## TASKS

**11** What does Source F show you about the attitude of some of the Petrograd press towards Lenin and the Bolsheviks?

**12** How important were the July Days to the Bolsheviks?
(For guidance on answering this type of question, see page 113.)

**13** Explain why Lenin used simple slogans to gain support.
(For guidance on answering this type of question, see page 90.)

**14** Describe the events of the Kornilov Revolt.
(For guidance on answering this type of question, see page 79.)

**15** Working in groups of three, explain why each of the following was important for the Bolsheviks in 1917: the April Theses (page 30), the July Days and the Kornilov Revolt.

**16** Study Source G. What is meant by the phrase 'victory over the counter-revolution'?

**17** Why was the Provisional Government in a risky position by October 1917? Answer by constructing a diagram as below, with the most important reasons at the top and moving in a clockwise direction.

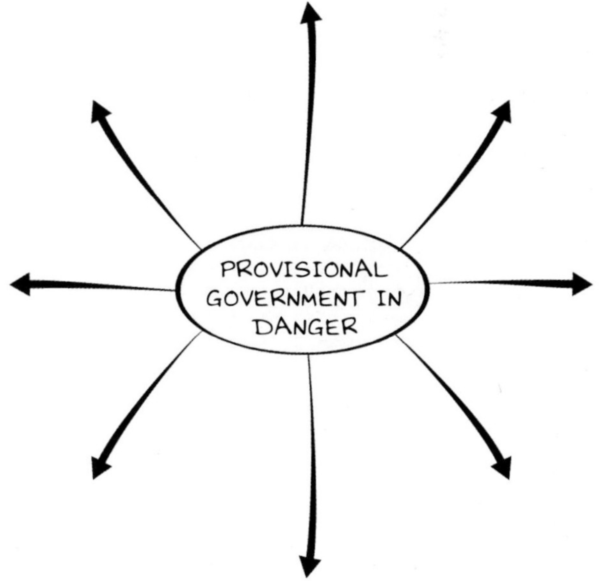


**18** Explain why the period of Dual Power resulted in weak government of Russia.
(For guidance on answering this type of question, see page 90.)

# How did the Bolsheviks seize power in October 1917?

The Bolsheviks began to grow in popularity in 1917 and during that year, membership of the Bolshevik Party had grown from 24,000 in February to 340,000 in October. In Petrograd alone the Bolsheviks had 60,000 members. Moreover, they had formed their own army – the Red Guard – which had been armed during the Kornilov Revolt.

## Lenin's decision to seize power

Following the Kornilov Revolt, the Bolsheviks were able to say that they were the true defenders of Petrograd. Above all, the Red Guard had retained the weapons given to them by Kerensky.

Lenin started calling for a revolution, but he still remained in exile in Finland. In September, he wrote 'History will not forgive us if we do not assume power.'

Lenin finally returned to Petrograd on 7 October and then went into hiding. On 10 October, Lenin persuaded the Bolshevik Central Committee to agree in principle to an uprising, but two influential leaders – Kamenev and Zinoviev – voiced strong objections. These two published their objections in a newspaper, alerting Kerensky to the imminent Bolshevik threat. Lenin was furious.

On 23 October, Kerensky tried to remove the Bolshevik threat – he closed down the Bolshevik papers (*Pravda* and *Izvestiya*) and attempts were made to round up leading Bolsheviks. The Bolsheviks were forced into action and Lenin ordered the revolution to begin before Kerensky could capture them. Thus, ironically, Kerensky had decided the exact timing of the revolution.

## The role of Trotsky

Trotsky was in exile at the time of the February Revolution. On his return to Russia in May 1917, he was concerned that many Mensheviks were supporting the Provisional Government. He was arrested in July as a result of his revolutionary activities and the following month he became an official Bolshevik Party member.

When the Bolsheviks secured control of the Petrograd Soviet, Trotsky was elected as its leader. Trotsky was the natural choice. He was a tireless activist and had been involved in the 1905 Revolution, had written extensively about Marxism and was a great speaker and motivator.

**Biography** Leon Trotsky 1879–1940

1879 Born Lev Davidovich Bronstein
1898 Arrested and spent four years in exile in Siberia
1902 Assumed the name Trotsky and joined the Social Democratic (SD) Party. Followed Martov and became a Menshevik
1905 Elected Chairman of the St Petersburg Soviet
1906 Exiled to Siberia but escaped after two years
1917 Returned to Russia in May. Split with the Mensheviks and joined the Bolshevik Party Chairman of Petrograd Soviet in September and member of the Military Revolutionary Committee (MRC)
1917 **Commissar** for Foreign Affairs
1918 Commissar for War
1927 Expelled from the Communist Party
1929 Deported from the Soviet Union
1940 Assassinated on the orders of Stalin in Mexico City

In October, he became the dominant member of the three-man **Military Revolutionary Committee (MRC)** of the Soviet. This provided a useful screen for his secret preparations. The MRC – in theory – controlled 20,000 Red Guards, 60,000 Baltic sailors and the 150,000 soldiers of the Petrograd garrison. Thus, in the event of an attack on Petrograd, the Bolsheviks would control not only the city's forces but the city itself.

From his office in the Smolny Institute, a building formerly used as a girls' school, Trotsky made his plans for the seizure of the key buildings of the Provisional Government.

In October, the Bolsheviks began to reduce their massive demonstrations and street skirmishes, because the crowds were not always easy to control. When they started preparing for the revolution, they began to rely more on small, disciplined units of soldiers and workers. The Bolsheviks, under the leadership of Trotsky, prepared for their overthrow of the Provisional Government on 24 October.

**Source A** From *Memoirs of a Revolutionary* by Victor Serge, 1945. Serge became a Bolshevik in 1919 but was expelled from the party in 1928 by Stalin for criticising his policies. Here he is writing about Trotsky's skills as a leader

*I first saw Trotsky at a packed meeting of the Petrograd Soviet. He was all tension and energy. He outshone Lenin through his oratorical talent, his organising ability, first with the army and then with the railways, and by his brilliant gift as a student of political theory ...*

**Source B** From *History of the Russian Revolution*, written by Trotsky in 1930. He was describing his time in the Smolny Institute during October 1917

*The Smolny Institute was being transformed into a fortress. In the top floor there were about two dozen machine-guns. All the reports about the movements of troops, the attitude of soldiers and workers, the agitation in the barracks, the happenings in the Winter Palace – all these came to the Smolny.*

## TASKS

1. Explain why Lenin decided to begin the revolution in October.
   (For guidance on answering this type of question, see page 90.)
2. What does Source A tell you about the character of Trotsky?
3. What information do Sources B and C provide about the importance of the Smolny Institute to the Bolshevik forces?
4. How useful is Source D to a historian studying the role of Trotsky?
   (For guidance on answering this type of question, see pages 59–60.)
5. Describe Trotsky's role in preparing the Bolsheviks in September and October for revolution.
   (For guidance on answering this type of question, see page 79.)

**Source C** Photograph of Bolsheviks outside the Smolny Institute, Petrograd, October 1917

**Source D** From an article by Joseph Stalin in *Pravda*, 6 November 1918. Stalin was a leading Bolshevik who was editor of *Pravda* and a member of the Bolshevik Central Committee

*All the work of practical organisation of the revolution was conducted under the immediate leadership of the Chairman of the Petrograd Soviet, Trotsky. It is possible to declare with certainty that the swift passing of the garrison to the side of the Soviet and the bold execution of the Military Revolutionary Committee, the party owes principally and above all to Comrade Trotsky.*

# What were the main events of the Bolshevik Revolution?

On the night of 24 October, Trotsky's plans were put into action. Key buildings were captured by the Bolsheviks, such as telegraph offices and railway stations, and roadblocks were set up on the city's bridges and surrounding the Winter Palace, where the Provisional Government was in session. There was little resistance and the citizens of Petrograd went about their everyday business.

Kerensky escaped from Petrograd on the morning of 25 October and tried to raise troops from the front, while the rest of the government remained in the Winter Palace. He could secure no further help. The troops guarding the Provisional Government – the Women's Battalion (known as the Amazons) and the military cadets – surrendered. When the cruiser *Aurora* sailed up the River Neva and fired its guns, the Provisional Government gave in and was placed under arrest. Some of its members were able to slip away unnoticed. In all, the actions of the day had ended with the death of six soldiers, eighteen arrests and the collapse of the Provisional Government.

**Source A** From a letter written by Lenin on the eve of the Bolshevik Revolution, 24 October. He was urging his colleagues to do what in fact they were doing!

*The situation is extremely critical. Delaying the uprising now really means death ... We must, at any price, tonight arrest the Ministers and we must disarm the military cadets ... We must not wait! We may lose everything! ... The government is tottering. We must deal it the death blow at any cost.*

**Source B** A scene from Sergei Eisenstein's film *October* which shows a re-enactment of the Bolsheviks storming the Winter Palace. The film was made in the Soviet Union in 1927 and was approved by the Communist government

**Source C** A. J. P. Taylor, a British historian, writing in his book *Revolutions and Revolutionaries*, published in 1980

*The Provisional Government had shrunk to a meeting of ministers in the Winter Palace. It was not overthrown by a mass attack on the Winter Palace. A few Red Guards climbed in through the servants' entrance, found the Provisional Government in a meeting and arrested the ministers in the name of the people. Six people, five of them Red Guards, were casualties of bad shooting by their own comrades.*

## The Bolsheviks take power

Meanwhile, the All-Russian Congress of Soviets was assembling at the Smolny Institute. The Bolsheviks held the most seats – 390 of 650. The Socialist Revolutionaries and Menshevik representatives condemned the Bolshevik takeover, because it was not a Soviet takeover of power. The two sets of representatives left the Congress and the Bolsheviks' position was immediately strengthened because of their huge majority.

The following day, 26 October, Lenin formed a government called the Council of People's Commissars. This had an all-Bolshevik membership:

- Lenin was the head of the government
- Trotsky was Commissar for Foreign Affairs
- Stalin was Commissar for Nationalities.

Within a week of the revolution in Petrograd, the Bolsheviks took control of Moscow and then began the work of securing control of the whole of Russia.

**Source D** An artist's interpretation of a poster, dated 5 November 1917, written by Lenin, announcing that the Bolsheviks had removed the Provisional Government

**To the Citizens of Russia!**

**The Provisional Government has been deposed. Power has passed into the hands of the Petrograd Soviet of Workers' and Soldiers' Deputies – the Military Revolutionary Committee, which leads the Petrograd proletariat and the garrison. The causes for which the people have fought – peace, the abolition of land ownership, workers' control over production and the establishment of Soviet power have been secured.**

**Long live the revolution of the workers, soldiers and peasants!**

## TASKS

1 Study Source A. What is the main message of Lenin's letter?

2 Why do Sources B and C have different views about the storming of the Winter Palace in October 1917? (In your answer you should refer to both the content of the sources and the authors.) (For guidance on answering this type of question, see pages 69–70.)

3 Study Source D. Why was Lenin careful to address the poster to 'workers, soldiers and peasants'?

4 Working in pairs, can you suggest reasons why there was so little opposition to the Bolshevik takeover in Petrograd in October 1917? Make a list of the reasons – you may find that many of them are also the reasons why there was a Bolshevik Revolution.

# Why were the Bolsheviks successful in October 1917?

## The role of Lenin

The role of Lenin in the success of the Bolshevik Revolution was crucial:

- He persuaded the Bolsheviks to oppose the war, unlike the Mensheviks and Socialist Revolutionaries, which was the key reason why Bolshevik support rose throughout 1917.
- He believed that a workers' revolution was possible, rather than many years away, unlike the Mensheviks and Socialist Revolutionaries who were prepared to follow Marx's idea that there had to be a bourgeois revolution before there could be a worker's revolution.
- He gave the Bolsheviks simple slogans, which were easily understood by the ordinary people. The slogans focused on the key issues which affected all of the ordinary people, for example 'Peace, Land, Bread'.
- He was primarily responsible for increasing membership of the party during the period that the Provisional Government was in office. He ensured that the message of the Bolsheviks was heard across Petrograd and Moscow by such means as political meetings, fliers and the newspaper *Pravda*.
- He created the Red Guard and used German money, which helped to equip them.
- He was a superb orator.
- He had tremendous energy and vitality and his commitment to revolution spurred on the Bolsheviks.

Moreover, Lenin persuaded the majority of the Central Committee to seize power in October. Trotsky organised the takeover, but without Lenin the Bolsheviks would not have even tried to remove the Provisional Government.

**Biography** Vladimir Illich Ulyanov ('Lenin') 1870–1924

| | |
|---|---|
| 1870 | Born Vladimir Illich Ulyanov |
| 1887 | Elder brother, Alexander, hanged as a conspirator in the attempted assassination of Tsar Alexander III |
| 1897 | Exiled to Siberia – adopted the name Lenin |
| 1902 | Wrote *What is to be Done?* in which he put forward the idea of the central role of dedicated party members in any revolution |
| 1903 | Led the Bolsheviks after the Social Democrat Party split into two groups |
| 1905 | Returned to Russia – played no part in the Revolution |
| 1906 | Exiled for much of the next eleven years |
| 1912 | Secured control of the Central Committee (the body responsible for making policies in the Bolshevik Party) |
| 1917 | Returned to Russia and led the Bolshevik Revolution |
| 1917–24 | Chairman of *Sovnarkom* |
| 1922 | Suffered two strokes and played little part in government thereafter |
| 1924 | Died 21 January |

**Source A**
A cartoon showing Lenin sweeping away his opponents. The caption reads 'Lenin cleans the earth of evil spirits'

## TASKS

1. How far does Source A support the view that the Bolshevik Revolution resulted in a complete change of government for Russia? (For guidance on answering this type of question, see pages 48–49.)
2. How important was Lenin to the success of the Bolshevik Revolution in October 1917? (For guidance on answering this type of question, see page 113.)

## The weaknesses of the Provisional Government

The Bolsheviks' success also relied on the weaknesses of the Provisional Government, which was only a temporary body before a Constituent Assembly could be elected. It had not been elected by the people. Moreover, it had had to share power in Petrograd with the Soviet from the beginning and could not overturn Soviet Order Number One (see page 28), which meant that it could not make any real long-term decisions about the future.

Kerensky was unable to remove the Bolsheviks completely from the political scene and during the Kornilov Revolt (see pages 32–33) he had actually armed them.

The Provisional Government was unable to retain the support of ordinary people in Petrograd. The continuation of the war, military defeats, the lack of food, inflation, the failure to deal with the land problem, successive strikes, and no sign of democratic elections all combined to seal the fate of Kerensky's government. In addition, the Bolsheviks were relentless in their publishing of so much propaganda that when the crisis came in October, Kerensky received little or no help from any quarter.

**Source B** From *Reaction and Revolution* by M. Lynch, a British historian, 1992

*The failure of the Provisional Government to rally effective military support in its hour of need was symptomatic of its much deeper failure over the previous eight months ... Kerensky's government came nowhere near to solving Russia's problems or satisfying her needs. Hence its support evaporated ... militarily disastrous, the Provisional Government was not considered to be worth struggling to save.*

## Bolshevik control of armed forces

Trotsky claimed that the Bolsheviks were successful because the soldiers of the Petrograd garrison did not side with the Provisional Government. Furthermore, the creation of the Military Revolutionary Committee enabled the Bolsheviks to control some of the armed forces at a critical time.

## Lack of alternatives

The many political parties did not offer clear leadership during 1917. They became discredited because they supported the continuation of the war. This led to discontent within the army and made it unreliable. The elections to the Constituent Assembly were delayed and the peasants' demand for land was not addressed. Consequently, anarchy and the seizing of land in the countryside increased as 1917 wore on, and **left-wing** agitators infiltrated the army and destroyed the morale of the soldiers.

**Source C** An extract from the diary of P. Sorokin, a Socialist Revolutionary describing the Bolshevik attack on the Provisional Government on 25 October 1917. The diary was published in 1920

*I learned that the Bolsheviks had brought up the warship Aurora and had opened fire on the Winter Palace, demanding the surrender of the members of the Provisional Government still barricaded there ... There was a regiment of women and young military trainees bravely resisting an overwhelming force of Bolshevik troops ... Poor women, poor lads, their situation was desperate, for we knew the wild sailors would tear them to pieces.*

### TASKS

**3** Use the information in Source B and your own knowledge to explain why the Provisional Government was not thought worthy of saving in October 1917.
(For guidance on answering this type of question, see page 40.)

**4** How useful is Source C to a historian studying the Bolshevik seizure of power?
(For guidance on answering this type of question, see pages 59–60.)

**5** Was the weakness of the Provisional Government the main reason for Bolshevik success in their seizure of power in October 1917?

In your answer you should:
- discuss the weaknesses of the Provisional Government as a factor helping the Bolsheviks to seize power
- discuss other factors which enabled the Bolsheviks to seize power in October 1917.

(For guidance on answering this type of question, see pages 101–2.)

# Examination guidance

This section provides guidance on how to answer a source comprehension question which is linked to the recall of your own knowledge. This is worth 4 marks.

Use the information in Source A and your own knowledge to explain why the Provisional Government faced problems during the autumn of 1917. (4 marks)

**Source A** From a school textbook

*Day by day the Provisional Government seemed to become more helpless and its control over events in Russia began to break down. The newspapers were filled with accounts of robberies and murders, showing that law and order had collapsed.*

## Tips on how to answer

- Read through the source, **underlining or highlighting** the key points.
- In your answer you should **try to rephrase and explain these points** in your own words.
- Aim to bring in your own **background knowledge** to expand upon these points.
- Think about any **other relevant factors** which are not included in the source and bring them into your answer.
- To obtain maximum marks **you need to do two things** – refer to information from the source and add to this with information from your own knowledge of this topic area.

### Response by candidate

*By the autumn of 1917 the Provisional Government seemed to have lost control of day-to-day events, causing its authority to weaken. Law and order on the streets had collapsed and there was an increase in violence and crime, which only added to the problems facing the Provisional Government. Its decision to continue the war was met with anger and a loss of support. There were massive food shortages which the Provisional Government seemed unable to solve. It also faced the problem of a rival to its power in the Petrograd Soviet which through Order No. One had control over Russia's armed forces. This only added to the problems facing the Provisional Government.*

Develops the information provided in the source, and begins to place it into context.

Identifies and explains other reasons why it faced problems.

**Examiner's comment**

This is a well-developed answer. The candidate demonstrates a sound understanding of this topic and has worked the source material well. There is a good blend of own knowledge to explain and expand on the information given in the source. There has been a clear attempt to identify other factors which caused problems for the Provisional Government. The answer is fully worthy of the maximum of 4 marks.

### Now you have a go

Use the information in Source B and your own knowledge to explain why the Kornilov Plot enabled the Bolsheviks to grow more powerful. (4 marks)

**Source B** From a school textbook

*As Kornilov and his forces approached Petrograd, Kerensky allowed the Bolshevik Red Guards to arm and was happy to see the Bolsheviks persuade many of Kornilov's troops to desert. Kerensky also set free many Bolsheviks who had been imprisoned after the July Days, so that there would be a considerable force to oppose Kornilov in Petrograd.*

# What were the consequences of the Revolutions of 1917?

**Source A** A Bolshevik poster issued soon after the October 1917 Revolution

The Bolsheviks had seized power with hardly any bloodshed. The Provisional Government melted away and Lenin was left to set up a government. However, the Bolsheviks did not have widespread support across Russia and Lenin was keen to impose his control on the country as soon as it was feasible.

Lenin faced the same problems as the Provisional Government had and he knew the most pressing problems were Russia's involvement in the war and the issue of land. In attempting to solve his problems, Lenin acted very quickly and the ***Sovnarkom***, the name given to the new government, passed several decrees in the hope of winning the support of the Russian people.

By March 1918, the war had been brought to a close and land had been redistributed among the peasants. However, Lenin had dissolved the new Constituent Assembly (parliament) and had begun to use the Bolsheviks' own secret police (the ***Cheka***).

**TASK**

What message is Source A trying to get across about the Bolshevik Revolution?

This chapter answers the following questions:

- How did the Bolsheviks establish the new Communist state?
- Why was the Treaty of Brest-Litovsk important?

**Examination guidance**

Throughout this chapter you will be given the opportunity to practise different exam-style questions and detailed guidance on how to answer an analysis and evaluation of a source question. This is worth 5 marks.

# How did the Bolsheviks establish the new Communist state?

## Problems facing Lenin in establishing a Bolshevik state

The government that Lenin set up in November 1917 was called *Sovnarkom*, short for Council of People's Commissars. *Sovnarkom* was made up solely of Bolsheviks because Lenin did not wish to share power with any of the other political parties. Lenin was Chairman of *Sovnarkom*, Trotsky was initially Commissar for Foreign Affairs but was appointed Commissar for War in 1918. Stalin was Commissar for Nationalities.

During the weeks after the Bolshevik takeover, soviets throughout Russia joined in the revolution and took over control of most towns and cities. By the end of 1917, nearly all Russia was in soviet hands. This did not mean that Lenin and the Bolsheviks had total control of Russia. Not all the soviets were run by Bolsheviks and, in the countryside, most peasants supported the Socialist Revolutionaries.

Even more awkward from Lenin's point of view, the Provisional Government had arranged for elections to be held in November for a new kind of parliament, called the Constituent Assembly. It seemed that the Socialist Revolutionaries would win more votes than the Bolsheviks. If that happened, the Bolsheviks would have to hand over control of *Sovnarkom* to their rivals. Lenin easily overcame this problem when the Constituent Assembly first met in January 1918. He sent in troops to dissolve it after only one day (see pages 44–45).

In addition to these problems, Lenin had to keep promises he had openly made in his April Theses (see page 30) – such as giving land to the peasants. If he failed to carry out his promises then Lenin knew that his support would diminish in the same way as had happened to Kerensky and the Provisional Government.

## The first decrees of *Sovnarkom*

*Sovnarkom* issued a series of decrees in November and December 1917 (see tables). It was these decrees which showed the Russian people that the Bolsheviks would keep their promises of 1917. Lenin had seen how support for the Provisional Government had withered away and he had no intention of this happening to the Bolsheviks. Importantly, Lenin ignored the Petrograd Soviet (which had members of the Mensheviks and Socialist Revolutionaries) in the first weeks after the revolution and relied only on *Sovnarkom*. *Sovnarkom* met twice each day and the power of the Soviet began to decline. This was Lenin's way of ensuring that the Bolsheviks had complete power. In addition, he set up the *Cheka* to remove potential and actual opponents (see page 44).

### November decrees

| Decree | Description |
|---|---|
| Decree on land | 220 million hectares of land taken from the tsar, the nobles, the Church and other landlords. Peasants to set up committees to divide the land fairly |
| Decree on unemployment insurance | Employment insurance to be introduced for all workers against injury, illness and unemployment |
| Decree on peace | *Sovnarkom* intended to make peace immediately with Russia's opponents in the war |
| Decree on work | An eight-hour day and a 40-hour week for all industrial workers to be introduced. There were restrictions on overtime and there was to be holiday entitlement for workers |
| Decree on titles | All titles and class distinctions were abolished. Women were declared equal to men |
| Decree on the press | All non-Bolshevik newspapers were banned |

December Decrees

| Decree | Description |
|---|---|
| Decree on workers' control | All factories to be placed under the control of elected committees of workers |
| Decree to set up the political police | The 'All-Russian Extraordinary Commission for Combating Counter-revolution and Sabotage' was formed – this became known as the *Cheka* (see page 44) |
| Decree on political parties | Russia's main liberal party, the Constitutional Democratic Party, was banned |
| Decree on banking | All banks in Russia came under *Sovnarkom*'s control |
| Decree on marriage | Couples were permitted to have non-religious weddings and divorce was made easier |

**Source A** From the Decree on Education, issued by *Sovnarkom* in 1917

*Every genuinely democratic power must in the sphere of education, make the removal of illiteracy and ignorance its first aim. It must acquire in the shortest time universal literacy by organising a network of schools and it must introduce universal, compulsory and free tuition for all.*

**Source B** From *The Communist Party of the Soviet Union*, published in 1963. The author, Leonard Schapiro, a British historian, was describing some of the first actions of the Bolshevik government

*Bolshevik practice within a few days of the removal of the Provisional Government was at variance with Lenin's repeated promises. He had said that when they were in power the Bolsheviks would guarantee to each political party which could gather enough supporters the facilities for publishing a newspaper. Some Socialist and Liberal papers, as well as Conservative papers were closed down in the first few days.*

## TASKS

**1** Describe the problems that Lenin faced when the Bolsheviks first took over in 1917.
(For guidance on answering this type of question, see page 79.)

**2** How useful is Source A to a historian studying how the Bolsheviks controlled Russia after 1917?
(For guidance on answering this type of question, see pages 59–60.)

**3** How far does Source B support the view that Lenin did not believe in democracy?
(For guidance on answering this type of question, see pages 48–49.)

**4** Look at the November and December Decrees. Copy the table below and fill it in to explain why each section in Russian society would support or oppose the decrees.

| Decree | Worker | Peasant | Middle classes | Nobility |
|---|---|---|---|---|
| | | | | |

**5** Working in pairs, look at the decrees passed by the Bolsheviks in November and December 1917 and discuss the following questions:

- Did Lenin follow the April Theses (see page 30)?
- In what ways might some people say that Lenin ruled like the tsar?

## The *Cheka*

In December 1917, Lenin used *Sovnarkom* to set up the 'All-Russian Extraordinary Commission for Combating Counter-revolution and Sabotage'. This became known as the *Cheka* and its head was Felix Dzerzhinsky. It was the Bolsheviks' secret police and was answerable directly to Lenin and he gave it unlimited powers. Initially, the *Cheka* had 100 operatives but by 1921 it had 30,000.

In March 1918, the *Cheka* based its headquarters in the Lubyanka in Moscow and organised itself in the following departments: counter-revolution, speculation, non-residents, and information. As the year progressed, the *Cheka* set up offices in soviets across the whole of Russia.

The purpose of the *Cheka* can be seen by its own clarification of those who it targeted:

- any civil or military servicemen suspected of working for Imperial Russia
- families of army officers (including children)
- any clergy
- workers and peasants who were under suspicion of not supporting the Soviet government
- any other person whose private property was valued at greater than 10,000 roubles.

Lenin and Dzerzhinsky used the *Cheka* to remove opponents of the Bolshevik regime and to shoot army deserters. Members of the main political parties – Cadets, Socialist Revolutionaries (SRs) and Mensheviks – were arrested and removed from political activities. Following the attempt on Lenin's life at the end of August, Dzerzhinsky began what became known as the **Red Terror**. By the end of 1918, the *Cheka* had 'removed' more than 50,000 people. It thus began to create a climate of fear and terror not only across Russia but even within the Bolshevik Party, making it difficult to criticise the new government. Hence the *Cheka* enabled Lenin and the Bolsheviks to retain power at a most difficult time.

## Why was the Constituent Assembly dissolved?

Elections were held for Russia's new parliament, the Constituent Assembly, in November 1917. They were the first free elections in Russian history. The Socialist Revolutionaries gained more seats in the Assembly than all the other parties put together (see the pie chart below).

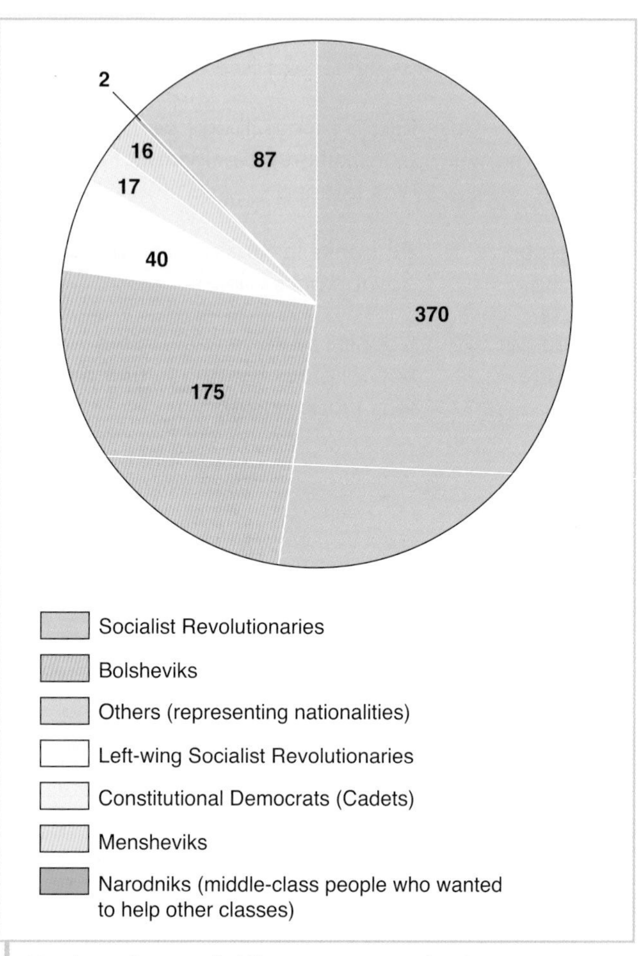


Number of seats of different parties in the Constituent Assembly, 1917. Total number of seats was 707

Lenin was concerned that the Bolsheviks had gained only a quarter of the votes and these were primarily from the working classes of the cities. He was also concerned that some of the nationalities, such as Finns and Estonians, were trying to break away and he wanted to avoid the disintegration of Russia.

Lenin wrote an article for *Pravda*, in which he stated that because there were soviets in Russia, there was no need for the Constituent Assembly. Nevertheless, the Constituent Assembly met on 18 January 1918. It would have the job of drawing up a new constitution for Russia. The Bolsheviks and the left-wing Socialist Revolutionaries proposed that the power of the Assembly be limited. When this was defeated, Lenin made his decision to dissolve it.

Fewer than 24 hours after the Assembly had met, Lenin gave the order to dissolve it. Bolshevik Red Guards killed and wounded more than 100 people who demonstrated in support of the Assembly outside the Tauride Palace. Two leaders of the Cadets were killed in a hospital. The Red Guards then prevented the elected deputies from entering the Assembly and closed it down permanently. Lenin had removed a threat to the Bolsheviks and *Sovnarkom* at a stroke.

**Source C** From a newspaper article written in 1948 by Victor Chernov, leader of the Socialist Revolutionary Party

*When we, the newly elected members of the Constituent Assembly, met on 18 January 1918, we found that the corridors were full of armed guards. Every sentence of my speech was met with outcries, some ironical, others accompanied by the waving of guns. Lenin lounged in his chair with the air of a man who was bored to death.*

**Source D** From the memoirs of Edgar Sissons written in 1931. Sissons was the US special representative in Russia in 1918

*The Constituent Assembly met in a ring of steel. Armed guards were all about us ... a line of guards stood or walked in the connecting corridor, and at every door was pair of sailors or soldiers. Even the ushers were armed men.*

**Source E** From an interview with C. Lindhagen, a Swedish eyewitness at the opening of the Constituent Assembly

*In one of the corridors a group of armed soldiers could be glimpsed. I was informed that several of the deputies (members) as well as the commissars were armed. I asked one of the commissars whether this was true. 'Of course' and he showed me the butt of a revolver in his pocket.*

## TASKS

**6** Explain why Lenin set up the *Cheka*.
(For guidance on answering this type of question, see page 90.)

**7** What do the election results tell us about the political situation in Russia at the beginning of 1918?

**8** How useful is Source C to a historian studying the reasons for the collapse of the Constituent Assembly?
(For guidance on answering this type of question, see pages 59–60.)

**9** What similarities and differences are there between Sources C, D and E in their views about the dissolution of the Constituent Assembly? To help you with this answer:

- make a copy of the following grid
- plan your answer using the grid.

| | C–D | D–E | C–E |
|---|---|---|---|
| Similarities | | | |
| Differences | | | |

**10** Explain why the Constituent Assembly was dissolved by Lenin.
(For guidance on answering this type of question, see page 90.)

# Why was the Treaty of Brest-Litovsk important?

## Lenin's decision to end Russia's involvement in the war

Lenin had opposed the war against Germany from the very beginning and much of the support the Bolsheviks had gained came from their opposition to the conflict. He was aware that if the Bolsheviks were to hold on to the power they had won in October 1917, then there would have to be an immediate peace settlement. He had seen how the war had firstly destroyed tsarism and then continued involvement cost the Provisional Government much support. Another important concern for Lenin was that prolonging the war could mean that the army would not continue to support him.

**Source A** German troops with the heaped-up bodies of dead Russian soldiers, early 1918

**Source B** Decree on Peace, issued by *Sovnarkom* in November 1917

*The workers' and peasants' government proposes to all the warring peoples and their governments that they enter immediately into talks for a just peace. This sort of peace would be an immediate one without seizure of foreign territory and without financial penalties.*

## Trotsky and the peace negotiations

Peace talks with Germany began on 3 December 1917 after an **armistice** with the **Central Powers** was agreed. Lenin sent Trotsky (Commissar for Foreign Affairs) as Russia's representative. Talks were held at Brest-Litovsk, near the German border. Trotsky and his negotiating team tried to prolong the talks as long as possible, because they believed that workers in central Europe were on the brink of revolution. When this revolution came, the war would end and then Germany and Russia would make a fair peace.

**Source C** Field Marshal Hindenburg, Germany's chief negotiator, writing about Trotsky at Brest-Litovsk

*Trotsky degraded the conference table to the level of a tub-thumper's street corner. Trotsky behaved more like a victor than vanquished, while trying to sow the seeds of political revolution in the ranks of our army.*

Initially, the German demands were so great that Trotsky walked out of the peace talks (General Skalon, one of the Russian negotiators, committed suicide on hearing the German terms) but Lenin insisted he return because he was aware that if the war continued then the Bolsheviks might not keep power.

Lenin's great fear was that German forces would march on Petrograd and overthrow the Bolshevik government. As the German army advanced into Russia in February 1918, Lenin's hand was forced and he decided to make peace. Trotsky was aware that the Russian army was unable to continue fighting because he had seen the dreadful state of its troops on his way to the negotiations. Trotsky dragged out negotiations with Germany and tried to follow his idea of 'no war no peace' but this only angered the German negotiators. When the Bolshevik Central Committee voted on the terms of the treaty, Trotsky abstained.

The treaty was signed on 3 March 1918. Trotsky refused to go to the final meeting.

## The terms of the Treaty of Brest-Litovsk

The terms of the treaty were extremely severe. Russia had to surrender huge tracts of land from the Black Sea to the Baltic. This amounted to about one million square kilometres and contained about 50 million people. In this territorial settlement, Germany gained parts of Poland and Russia's Baltic states (Estonia, Latvia and Lithuania) and Turkey was awarded parts of the Caucasus region. The Russian provinces of Finland, Ukraine and Georgia were given independence.

Within the ceded territory, Russia lost 27 per cent of its arable land, 26 per cent of its railways and 74 per cent of its iron ore and coal. Finally, Russia had to pay reparations amounting to three billion roubles. The impact on Russia's economy would be immense.

Lenin was heavily criticised by many Bolsheviks and by the Socialist Revolutionaries. For Lenin, Russia's suffering was a small price to pay for the coming world socialist revolution. Lenin won the debate in the Bolshevik Party about accepting the terms of the treaty but only by the narrowest of margins. Some Bolsheviks such as Bukharin, a member of the Bolshevik Central Committee, wanted to continue the war to try and bring about the end of the German Empire.

**Source D** Lenin speaking to fellow Bolsheviks in March 1918 about the Treaty of Brest-Litovsk

*Our impulse tells us to refuse to sign this robber peace ... Russia can offer no physical resistance because she is materially exhausted by three years of war ... The Russian Revolution must sign the peace to obtain a breathing space to recuperate for the struggle.*

## The end of the First World War

Lenin's decision to make peace was a huge gamble because he made the treaty on the assumption that ultimately Germany would be defeated in the war and this was by no means certain when the Treaty of Brest-Litovsk was signed. The decision seemed to have been a terrible mistake when the Germans launched their Spring Offensive on the Western Front. The German attack saw the biggest breakthrough in three years of warfare on the Western Front. The offensive was astonishing in terms of the land it won, but it had been extremely expensive in terms of men lost. However, because of the speed of its advance, supplying the German forces became very difficult and the attack ground to a halt.

The arrival of thousands of US troops after April 1918 began to swing the war to the Allies' favour and they launched their Summer Offensive in August. On the first day, the Germans retreated some 320 kilometres and during September, Germany's allies began to seek ceasefires with the Allied forces. Germany's military leaders now realised they could not win the war. At the same time, there were political upheavals within Germany and by early November the government of Germany concluded an armistice with the Allies.

With the ending of the war in Europe in November 1918, the Treaty of Brest-Litovsk became meaningless. The defeat of Germany now meant that the treaty had no legality. However, the treaty had given Lenin and his government valuable breathing space to consolidate itself. Yet, just as the major danger of Germany was removed, Lenin had to face serious internal threats and, by the spring of 1918, Russia was convulsed by civil war.

### TASKS

1. What does Source A tell you about why many Russians wanted to end the war with Germany? (For guidance on answering this type of question, see page 22.)
2. How useful is Source B to a historian studying the reasons why Russia left the war in 1917? (For guidance on answering this type of question, see pages 59–60.)
3. How far does Source C support the view that Trotsky was against making peace with Germany? (For guidance on answering this type of question, see pages 48–49.)
4. Describe the main terms of the Treaty of Brest-Litovsk. (For guidance on answering this type of question, see page 79.)
5. Use the information in Source D and your own knowledge to explain why Lenin was prepared to accept the terms of the Treaty of Brest-Litovsk. (For guidance on answering this type of question, see page 40.)

# Examination guidance

This section provides guidance on how to answer a source analysis and evaluation question which is linked to the recall of your own knowledge. This is worth 5 marks.

How far does Source A support the view that Russia was harshly treated under the terms of the Treaty of Brest-Litovsk? (5 marks)

**Source A** A map showing the terms imposed on Russia by the Treaty of Brest-Litovsk which was signed in March 1918

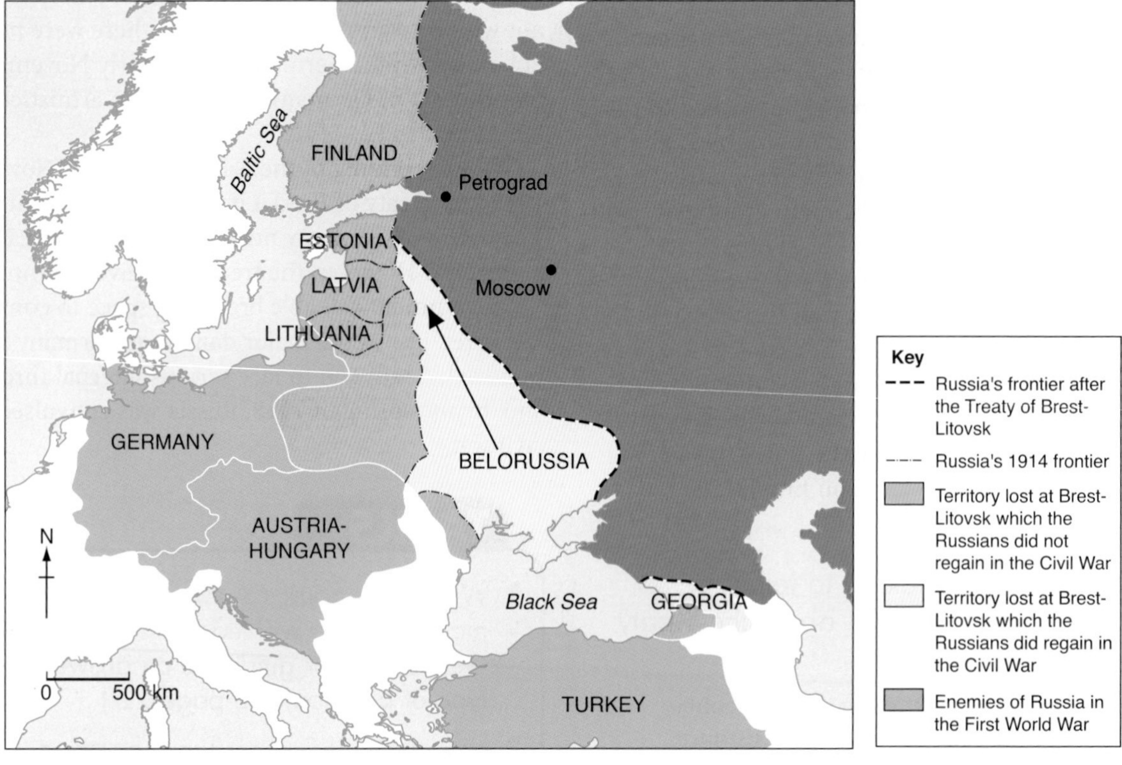


## Tips on how to answer

- This question can relate to a visual or a written source.
- If it is a visual source you should aim to pick out relevant details from what you can see in the illustration and, equally importantly, from the caption which supports the source. It is useful to scribble notes around the source.
- If it is a written source you should underline or highlight the key points.
- In your answer you should use these details, explaining them in your own words and linking them directly to the question.
- You should bring in your own knowledge of this topic to expand on these points and to provide additional material which is not provided in the source.
- To obtain maximum marks you must remember to give a reasoned judgement which addresses the question; for example, 'This source does/does not support the view that … because …'.

## Response by candidate

*The source supports the view that Russia was harshly treated because it shows that the price Russia paid for leaving the war was very high. The Germans demanded that Russia give up Finland, the Baltic regions of Latvia, Lithuania and Estonia, the region of Russian Poland and the Ukraine. In total Russia lost 50 million people which confirms that it was a harsh settlement. Some Russians wanted to reject the treaty and carry on fighting. What is not recorded in the source is that Russia was forced to pay war damages of three billion roubles which was a large sum of money. Such harsh terms were a cause of the outbreak of Civil War in 1919. Source A therefore contains considerable detail to show that the treatment of Russia under the terms of the peace treaty was very harsh.*

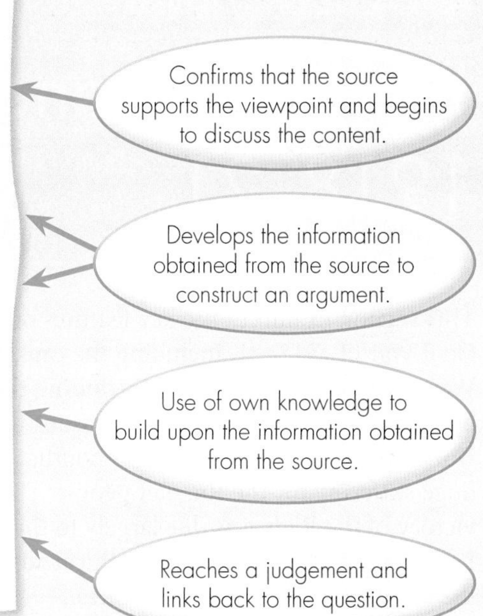


### Examiner's comment

A developed answer which makes good use of the map and its key. The candidate expands on the content of the source, explaining key details and supplies background knowledge to illustrate them, for example stating that the terms were so harsh that many Russians wanted to reject them and continue fighting. The reference to a damage payment of three billion roubles provided context through the inclusion of own knowledge. This is an informed and reasoned evaluation with a good supported judgement linked directly to the question. It is worthy of the maximum of 5 marks.

## Now you have a go

How far does Source B support the view that the Bolsheviks were not in a strong position following the election results of November 1917? (5 marks)

**Source B** Lenin was forced to hold Russia's first free elections in November 1917 to elect members to a Constituent Assembly. The table gives the results of this election

| Party | Seats in Constituent Assembly |
|---|---|
| Socialist Revolutionaries | 370 |
| Bolsheviks | 175 |
| Left Socialist Revolutionaries (supporters of Bolsheviks) | 40 |
| Cadets | 17 |
| Mensheviks | 16 |
| Others | 89 |

This section examines the key features of the Russian Civil War of 1918–21, including the causes of the Civil War, the two sides in the war including the part played by foreign intervention and the reasons for the eventual **Bolshevik** victory. It was a bitter conflict that caused huge suffering for the Russian people. The eventual victory of the Reds was due largely to the leadership of Lenin and Trotsky, their geographical advantages and the many weaknesses of the Whites.

Each chapter explains a key issue and examines important lines of enquiry as outlined below:

**Chapter 4**: What were the principal causes of the Civil War?

- Why was there economic hardship across Russia?
- Why was there opposition to the Bolsheviks?
- Who were the rival factions that opposed the Bolsheviks?

**Chapter 5**: Who were the main sides in the Civil War?

- What part was played by the White Generals in the Civil War?
- What part was played by foreign powers in the Civil War?
- What was the role of Trotsky and the Red Army in the Civil War?
- What happened to the tsar and his family?

**Chapter 6**: Why were the Reds able to win the Civil War?

- What were the strengths of the Reds?
- What were the weaknesses of the Whites?

**Source A** A Bolshevik poster of 1918. It shows the sword of the Red Army cutting off the advance of the White armies

## TASK

What can you learn from Source A about the two sides in the Civil War?

# What were the principal causes of the Civil War?

The Bolsheviks faced opposition from a variety of groups following their takeover in October 1917. This culminated in a civil war which lasted from 1918 to 1921. This opposition came about because of food shortages, the introduction of **War Communism** and the Treaty of Brest-Litovsk. The two sides in this war were known as the Reds, the supporters of the Bolsheviks, and the Whites, which included supporters of the tsar, the **Socialist Revolutionaries** (**SRs**) and countries such as the USA, Britain and France.

This chapter answers the following questions:

- Why was there economic hardship across Russia?
- Why was there political opposition to the Bolsheviks?
- Who were the rival factions that opposed the Bolsheviks?

**TASK**

How useful is Source A to a historian studying the events of the Civil War?
(For guidance on answering this type of question, see pages 59–60.)

**Examination guidance**

Throughout this chapter you will be given the opportunity to practise different exam-style questions and detailed guidance on how to answer an analysis and evaluation of the utility of a source question. This is worth 6 marks.

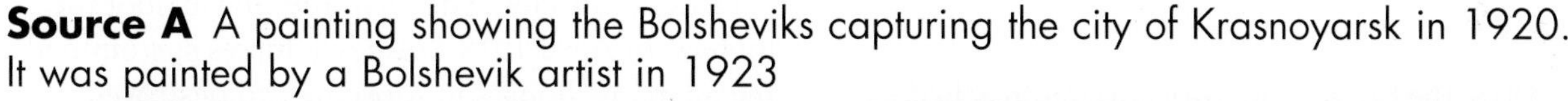

**Source A** A painting showing the Bolsheviks capturing the city of Krasnoyarsk in 1920. It was painted by a Bolshevik artist in 1923

# Why was there economic hardship across Russia?

One of the main reasons for opposition to the Bolsheviks was the economic and social hardship in the months after the October Revolution.

## Food shortages

In the six months following the October Revolution, the Bolsheviks had failed to deal with the country's most pressing need, food shortages and starvation, especially in the towns and cities. This was an important reason for the growth of opposition to the Bolsheviks. Reasons for food shortages were as follows:

- Problems of distribution. The railway system had virtually collapsed due to fuel shortages and could not cope with the transportation of foodstuffs to the cities.
- Problems of inflation. Peasants were unwilling to sell foodstuffs for paper money due to the loss of value of the currency. Many peasants used their grain to fatten their cattle, or sold it to **black market** traders from the towns. Many others turned it into vodka.
- Problems of production. Russia's main wheat-supply area, the Ukraine, had been annexed by the Germans under the terms of the Treaty of Brest-Litovsk in March 1918 (see page 46). Grain supplies were over 13 million tonnes short of the nation's needs.

In March 1918, the bread ration in Petrograd reached its lowest ever allocation of 50 grams per day. Hunger drove many industrial workers out of the major industrial cities. By June 1918, the workforce in Petrograd had shrunk by 60 per cent and the overall population had declined by between two and three million.

**Source A** An eyewitness account by a British refugee from Petrograd, 1918, who was writing to his family in England

*It is a common occurrence when a horse falls down in the street for the people to cut off the flesh of the animal the moment it has breathed its last. Another way of getting food was by buying it at excessive prices from members of the* ***Red Guard*** *who are well fed.*

**Source B** From *Memoirs of a Revolutionary* by Victor Serge, 1945. Serge became a Bolshevik in 1919 but was expelled from the party in 1928 by Stalin for criticising his policies. Here he is describing rationing in Petrograd in 1918

*The rations were minute: black bread, a few herrings each month, a very small quantity of sugar for people in the 'first category' (workers and soldiers) and none at all for the 'third category' (non-workers). Last winter was torture – no heating, no lighting and the ravages of famine.*

## Violence on the streets

These dire circumstances in the towns and cities led to growing violence on the streets and encouraged open challenges to the Bolsheviks.

- One such challenge came from an **anarchist** group known as the Black Guard who had roamed the countryside and large cities taking over buildings and the homes of the well-to-do, including 25 palaces in Moscow. They had the slogan 'loot the looters'. In April 1918 Bolshevik forces surrounded the anarchist houses in Moscow and destroyed their headquarters.
- The Socialist Revolutionaries, who had been driven from the government following their refusal to accept the Treaty of Brest-Litovsk, attempted a takeover in May 1918. This failed but they continued to carry out terrorist activities. There were two unsuccessful assassination attempts against Lenin in July and August 1918, while two Bolshevik Party bosses were assassinated during the same period.

**Source C** A photograph taken in the summer of 1918. It shows scuffles in a street in Moscow between the Bolsheviks and the Socialist Revolutionaries

## War Communism

The measures that Lenin and the Communists took to keep the army supplied during the Civil War became known as War Communism. War Communism was not one particular law passed by the Bolsheviks. It was a whole series of laws or measures by which the government took control over the economy. It was brought in to deal with the food shortages but made the situation worse. It was a very unpopular policy which provoked even more widespread opposition to the Bolsheviks in towns, cities and the countryside.

## TASKS

1 How useful is Source A to an historian studying the situation in Petrograd in 1918? (For guidance on answering this type of question, see pages 59–60.)

2 Use the information in Source B and your own knowledge to explain why conditions were hard in the towns in 1918. (For guidance on answering this type of question, see page 40.)

3 Describe the challenges to the Bolsheviks in Moscow in 1918. (For guidance on answering this type of question, see page 79.)

4 Study Source C. Put together a Bolshevik caption for this photograph.

5 Imagine you are a British journalist reporting about conditions in Petrograd in June 1918. Put together a newspaper headline for your article.

# Why was there opposition to the Bolsheviks?

As well as economic problems leading to challenges to the Bolsheviks, they faced opposition from different parts of Russian society. This was for a number of other reasons including the reforms they introduced, the dissolution of the **Constituent Assembly**, and the signing of the Treaty of Brest-Litovsk.

## Lenin's reforms

In the first months after the October Revolution, Lenin passed a series of decrees which did encourage support from town workers and peasants but alienated other groups.

| Decree | Description | Opposition |
|---|---|---|
| Decree on land | 540 million acres of land taken from the tsar, the nobles, the Church and other landlords | The nobles, other landlords and the Church whose land was seized. Many of these supported the Whites during the Civil War |
| Decree on peace | Announced that the Bolsheviks intended to make peace immediately with Russia's opponents in the war | Nationalists who wanted to continue the war and objected to the huge loss of land to the Germans. Many fought against the Bolsheviks in the Civil War |
| Decree on titles | All titles and class distinctions were abolished | Nobles who lost their privileged position and fought against the Bolsheviks during the Civil War |
| Decree on the press | All non-Bolshevik newspapers were banned | Other political parties such as the Socialist Revolutionaries whose views were censored. They supported the Whites during the Civil War |
| Decree to set up the political police | The 'All-Russian Extraordinary Commission for Combating Counter-revolution and Sabotage' was formed, known as the ***Cheka*** (see page 94) | This was seen as no different from the repression of the tsars when it carried out a policy of **Red Terror** in 1918, especially after assassination attempts on Lenin |
| Decree on banking | All banks in Russia came under the control of the government | Bankers and industrialists who lost their wealth and businesses and supported the opponents of the Bolsheviks |

## The Constituent Assembly

The decision to dissolve the Constituent Assembly in 1918 did not win the Bolsheviks any friends (see page 44). The Socialist Revolutionaries and **Cadets** accused the Bolsheviks of seizing power by force and demanded the re-calling of the Assembly. The other political parties, especially the Socialist Revolutionaries who had a majority in the Assembly, were furious with the Bolsheviks and eventually supported the Whites during the Civil War.

## Reactions to the Treaty of Brest-Litovsk

As we have seen in Chapter 3 (page 47), the Treaty of Brest-Litovsk was signed in March 1918. The treaty greatly increased the opposition to the Bolsheviks. Patriotic Russians were horrified by the terms. Giving away large chunks of the Russian homeland antagonised many Russians, irrespective of class or party, and encouraged them to join anti-Bolshevik groups. It even caused splits in the Bolshevik Party. Bukharin, a leading Bolshevik and editor of ***Pravda***, the Bolshevik Party newspaper, and the **left wing** of the party saw it as a shameful peace which helped Germany to survive as an imperial power.

People objected to the Treaty because of the following reasons:

- the dictated nature of the peace
- the way in which Lenin and Trotsky were prepared to sacrifice national interest to secure peace almost at any price
- the amount of land and population lost (see page 47)
- the amount of reparations (see page 47).

**Source A** From *With the German Guns, Fifty Months on the Western Front, 1914–1918* by Herbert Sulzbach, 1935. Herbert Sulzbach was a German representative at Brest-Litovsk. This is an extract from his diary dated 3 March 1918

*The final peace treaty has been signed with Russia. Our conditions are hard and severe, but our quite exceptional victories entitle us to demand these, since our troops are nearly in Petersburg, and further over on the southern front, Kiev has been occupied, while in the last week we have captured the following men and items of equipment: 6800 officers, 54,000 men, 2400 guns, 5000 machine-guns, 8000 railway trucks, 8000 locomotives, 128,000 rifles and two million rounds of artillery ammunition.*

### TASKS

1. Explain why the dissolution of the Constituent Assembly increased opposition to the Bolsheviks.
(For guidance on answering this type of question, see page 90.)
2. How important was the signing of the Treaty of Brest-Litovsk in increasing opposition to the Bolsheviks?
(For guidance on answering this type of question, see page 113.)
3. Use information from Source A and your own knowledge to explain why the Bolsheviks signed the Treaty of Brest-Litovsk.
(For guidance on answering this type of question, see page 40.)
4. Put together a mind map summarising the main economic and political reasons for the growth of opposition to the Bolsheviks. Rank these reasons in order clockwise, beginning with the most important at 12 o'clock.

# Who were the rival factions that opposed the Bolsheviks?

Growing opposition to the Bolsheviks caused by economic hardship and Lenin's reforms hardened into civil war in the early summer of 1918. There were a number of different factions involved in the civil war against the Bolsheviks including:

- the Czech Legion
- the Whites
- the Greens
- foreign powers.

Each had different aims and support.

## The Czech Legion

There is no specific date for the start of the Civil War but, by May 1918, events escalated when the Czech Legion revolted. The Czech Legion was a group of about 42,000 soldiers who had volunteered to fight on the Russian side in the First World War as a means of gaining independence from Austria-Hungary. They found themselves isolated after the Treaty of Brest-Litovst and formed themselves into the Czech Legion. The Allies convinced the Bolsheviks to withdraw the Czech Legion from their crumbling front and ship them via train 6000 miles across Russia to Vladivostok. From here they would be transported by sea to the **Western Front** and rejoin the Allies (Britain, France and the USA) in the hope of winning international support for the formation of an independent state of Czechoslovakia.

The presence of this well-equipped foreign army making its way across Russia was not welcome to the Bolsheviks. Local **soviets** began to challenge the Czech Legion and there was fierce fighting during its progress along the Trans-Siberian railway. At the railway station of Cheliabinsk, a Hungarian prisoner of war threw an iron bar at a Czech and badly hurt him. A fight broke out and several Czechs were arrested by the local soviet. The rest of the furious Czech troops rebelled and took over the Trans-Siberian railway. All this encouraged the Whites to come out openly against the Bolshevik regime.

**Source A** Czech troops on top of an armoured train on the Trans-Siberian railway in 1919

## The Whites

The Whites was the collective name for those who opposed the Bolsheviks (the Reds). They consisted of:

- Former tsarists, nationalists, nobles, landowners and wealthy industrialists who wanted the restoration of the tsar.
- Liberals and moderate socialists who wanted the Bolsheviks defeated and law and order re-established.
- Socialist Revolutionaries who wanted the restoration of the Constituent Assembly.

The Whites had some military support from ex-tsarist officers and were in a position to fight the Bolsheviks. For example, there was General Deniken in the Caucasus, General Yudenich in Estonia and Admiral Kolchak in Siberia. The Czech Legion gave its support to the White generals.

**Source B** A Proclamation of the Whites to the Workers and Peasants, 8 July 1918

*The Soviet of People's* ***Commissars*** *has brought ruin to Russia. Instead of bread and peace it has brought famine and war. The Soviet of the People's Commissars has made of mighty Russia a bit of earth dripping with the blood of peaceful citizens doomed to the pangs of hunger. They are arresting and shooting workers who do not agree with their policies, are manipulating the elections, and are strangling all civil liberties. To arms, all! Down with the Soviet People's Commissars. Only by overthrowing it shall we have bread, peace and freedom.*

## The Greens

These were groups who refused to be conscripted into the official White armies. They included the following:

- Peasant armies often made up of deserters from other armies. They were generally little more than groups of bandits who did well out of raiding and looting their neighbours. They wanted an end to War Communism.
- National minorities, for example, the Georgians, who saw an opportunity to establish their independence from Russia. If the Bolsheviks were weak and could be attacked on many fronts, then independence was a possibility. The most famous was the Green Army of Nestor Makhno which used **guerrilla** tactics to fight for the independence of the Ukraine.

## TASKS

1. Use the information in Source A and your own knowledge to explain why the actions of the Czech Legion sparked the Civil War. (For guidance on answering this type of question, see page 40.)
2. How far does Source B support the view that the Bolshevik government had ruined Russia? (For guidance on answering this type of question, see pages 48–49.)
3. How useful is Source C to an historian studying why foreign powers intervened in the Civil War? (For guidance on answering this type of question, see pages 59–60.)

## Foreign powers

Allied troops had been sent to Russia in 1918 to help to reopen the Eastern Front against Germany. However, before they could go into action the war ended in November 1918. The troops remained in Russia to guard munitions dumps in Archangel and Murmansk.

Britain, France, the USA and Japan were all determined to prevent the spread of communism and intervened in the war to support the Whites. This was for several reasons:

- Lenin had withdrawn from the war and signed the Treaty of Brest-Litovsk.
- The Bolsheviks cancelled payments of all loans given by the Allies to Russia.
- Britain, France and the USA feared the spread of communism to their own countries.

**Source C** From a speech made by Lenin to leading Bolsheviks, January 1919

*England, France and America are waging war against Russia. They are avenging themselves on the Soviet Union for having overthrown the landowners and capitalists and they are aiding and abetting the Russian landowners with money and military supplies. They, in turn, are mounting an attack against Soviet power from Siberia, the Don and the northern Caucasus in an attempt to restore the tsar, the landowners and the capitalists. But no! This shall never be.*

**Source D** A Bolshevik poster of 1918 showing the Red Army fighting a many-headed monster which represents the different groups that opposed Lenin, including the tsar

## TASKS

**4** What does Source D show you about opposition to the Bolsheviks during the Civil War? (For guidance on answering this type of question, see page 22.)

**5** Which group posed the most serious threat to the Bolsheviks? Make a copy of the concentric circles. Rank the different groups who opposed the Bolsheviks in order beginning with the most serious in the centre circle. Explain your decision.

**6** Was hunger the main reason for the outbreak of the Civil War?

In your answer you should:

- discuss the impact of hunger as a cause of the outbreak of the Civil War
- discuss other factors that contributed to the outbreak of the Civil War.

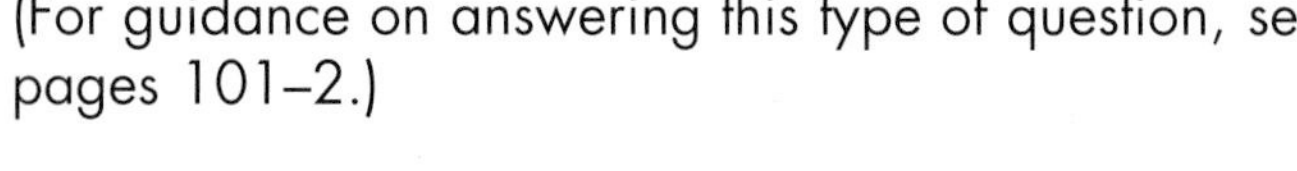

(For guidance on answering this type of question, see pages 101–2.)

## Examination guidance

This section provides guidance on how to answer an analysis and evaluation of the utility of a source question. This is worth 6 marks.

How useful is Source A to the historian studying the reasons why some foreign powers joined the Civil War in Russia? Explain your answer using the source and your own knowledge. (6 marks)

There are two candidate responses to this question, one below and one on page 60.

**Source A** Claire Baker, a British historian, writing in a GCSE history textbook, *Russia 1917–1945*, published in 1990

*Russia's former allies, angered by the Bolshevik withdrawal from the First World War, quickly offered to help the White opposition, and the Whites in turn promised to support the war against Germany. Anger over the war, and fears about the possible spread of communism to other capitalist countries, were used to justify further intervention in Soviet affairs by foreign powers after Germany's collapse in 1918.*

### Tips on how to answer

This question will involve the analysis and evaluation of a primary or secondary source.

- In your answer you will need to evaluate the usefulness of this source in terms of its **content**, its **origin** and its **purpose**.

| **Content** | **Origin** | **Purpose** |
|---|---|---|
| What does the source say? | Who said it? When did they say it? | Why was it said? Who was it said to and why? Is it biased? |

- You should aim to write about two to three sentences about the content of the source, putting the information into your own words and supporting it with your own knowledge of this topic.
- You should then comment on the author of the source, noting when the source was written and under what circumstances.
- You should consider why the source was written and whether this makes the source biased. Remember that a biased source can still be very useful to the historian and so do not just dismiss it.
- To obtain maximum marks your answer must contain reasoned comments on each of the three COP elements (content, origin, purpose). If you only write about the content of the source do not expect to get more than half marks.

### Response by candidate one

<u>This source was written by Claire Baker in 1990. It is useful because it says that the foreign powers were angry that the Bolsheviks had taken Russia out of the war against Germany.</u> The foreign powers also feared that communism would spread to other countries. They wanted to stop this from happening and were ready to help take action against the Bolsheviks. <u>This information is therefore very useful to a historian.</u>

Paraphrases the attribution but offers no further development.

Begins to discuss the content but there is little development. There is some own knowledge but it is limited.

A comment that lacks support.

Examiner's comment: The candidate has attempted two aspects of COP – the **content** and to a much lesser extent the **origin**. Much of the reference to the content is paraphrased and there has been little attempt to develop the material or explain it. There is a brief display of own knowledge. The origin is not developed and is just a paraphrase of the attribution. There is no attempt to consider the purpose. The candidate needs to consider why the source was written and under what circumstances. The answer reaches low level two and scores half marks, 3 out of 6.

## Response by candidate two

*Source A is very useful to historians because it says that those countries which had fought on the same side as Russia in the First World War were angry that the Bolsheviks had agreed to peace terms with Germany. They were prepared to help the Whites in their struggle with the Bolsheviks as the Whites promised to bring Russia back into the war against Germany. This would force Germany to fight on more than one front. These same foreign powers were also very worried that Communist ideas would spread outside Russia to other countries and they wanted to stop this. They did not want a repeat of such revolutions. The source comes from a GCSE history textbook which was written in 1990. Its author, the historian Claire Baker, was writing over 70 years after the event. She would have had the benefit of hindsight and will have had the opportunity to research her work and reflect on what has been written by other historians and contemporaries on this subject. The information is likely to be reliable as it would have been researched. As it was written for educational purposes it is unlikely to be biased in its interpretation. However, a GCSE study would not have gone into this topic area in any depth.*

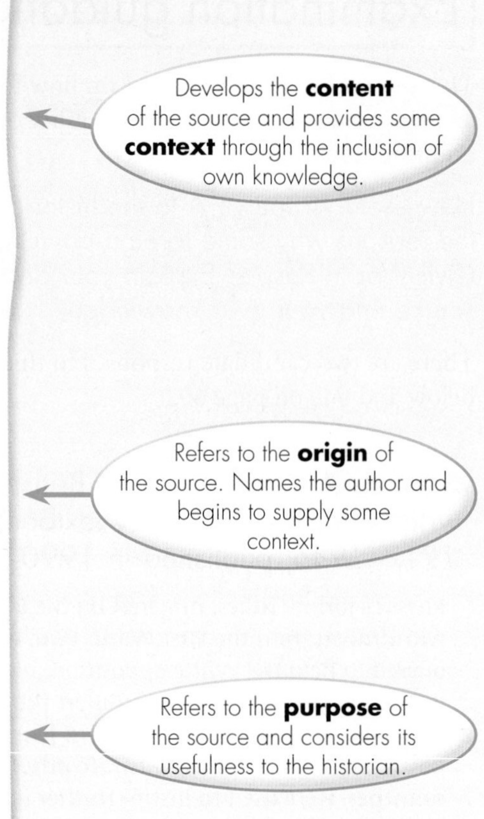


### Examiner's comment

This is an informed answer in which the candidate demonstrates good knowledge and understanding. The content of the source has been explained well and contextualised through the inclusion of own knowledge. Reference has been made to the desire of the foreign powers to bring Russia back into the war and also to stop the possible spread of Bolshevik ideas to other countries. The origin of the source is clearly identified, and there was been a good attempt to consider the purpose, spelling out its educational value and usefulness as a piece of historical research. This is a rounded COP evaluation which reaches the highest level and is worthy of the maximum of 6 marks.

# Who were the main sides in the Civil War?

The Russian Civil War lasted for almost three years (1918–21) and involved many groups. The Bolsheviks faced threats from various armies, including the White armies of Yudenich, Denikin and Kolchak and the Green Army of Makhno. These threats were supplemented by intervention in the form of armed forces and supplies from foreign powers such as Britain, France, the USA and Japan. However, these formidable threats were successfully met due to the leadership of Trotsky, who set up a strong force known as the Red Army. Moreover, the murder of the tsar and his family removed the main focal point for the opponents of the Bolsheviks.

This chapter answers the following questions:

- What part was played by the White Generals in the Civil War?
- What part was played by foreign powers in the Civil War?
- What was the role of Trotsky and the Red Army in the Civil War?
- What happened to the tsar and his family?

**Examination guidance**

Throughout this chapter you will be given the opportunity to practise different exam-style questions and detailed guidance on how to answer a historical interpretation through the analysis, evaluation and cross-referencing of two sources question. This is worth 8 marks.

**Source A** A selection of Trotsky's orders to the Red Army, 1918

- *Every scoundrel who incites anyone to retreat, to desert, or not fulfil a military order will be shot.*
- *Every soldier of the Red Army who voluntarily deserts his post, will be shot.*
- *Every soldier who throws away his rifle or sells part of his equipment will be shot.*
- *Those guilty of harbouring deserters are liable to be shot.*
- *Houses in which deserters are found are liable to be burned down.*

**TASK**

What can you learn from Source A about the Red Army?

# What part was played by the White Generals in the Civil War?

At first, the Civil War did not go well for the Reds. They suffered defeat after defeat in 1918 and early 1919 and were attacked on all sides by White armies led by experienced commanders and supported by foreign powers:

- General Yudenich, with British support, attacked from the north-west and threatened Petrograd.
- General Deniken, supported mainly by the French, threatened the south.
- With British support, Admiral Kolchak attacked from the east.

However, in 1919 the tide began to turn.

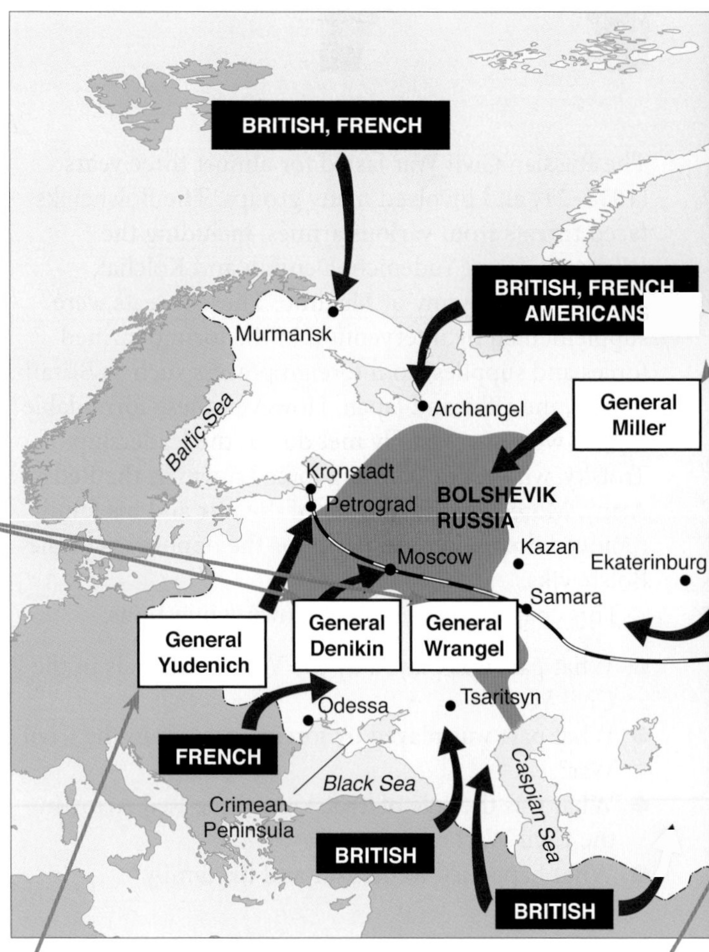


### White Generals Denikin and Wrangel in the south

Denikin had an army of 150,000 which included a great number of **Cossacks** from the Don region. His army advanced through the Don region and aimed to link up with Kolchak's army in the east. By the summer of 1918, Denikin's army was besieging Tsaritsyn, which was vital to the Reds in order to protect grain supplies and prevent the link between the southern and eastern White armies. It was successfully defended by the Bolsheviks under the leadership of Stalin.

Denikin launched another offensive in 1919 which got to within 320 km of Moscow. It was defeated by a Red counter-attack led by Trotsky and driven back to the Crimean Peninsula. Denikin was replaced by Wrangel, who held out until the following November 1920 when he was evacuated by British and French ships.

### White General Yudenich in the west

General Yudenich's army was the smallest army, only some 15,000, and it reached the outskirts of Petrograd in October 1919 with the support of Estonian troops who wanted independence from Russia. However, Yudenich failed to secure the Petrograd railway, which enabled the Bolsheviks to send in massive reinforcements to prevent the fall of the city to White forces. The Bolsheviks also secured a separate **armistice** with Estonian forces by promising to recognise Estonian independence. Without the support of Estonia, Yudenich dissolved his armies in mid-1920.

### White Admiral Kolchak in the east

Admiral Kolchak led an army of about 140,000 which advanced from the east, supported by the Czech regiment. At first he was very successful and, by June 1919, had captured Kazan and Samara. However, by the autumn of 1919 the Red Army had forced Kolchak to retreat and in the following year he was captured and shot. This defeat was due to the determined counter-attacks by the Red Army as well as differences and quarrels with the Czechs.

### White General Miller in the north

After the Bolshevik takeover, Miller, a general in the tsarist army, fled to Archangel and declared himself Governor-General of Northern Russia. In May 1919 Admiral Kolchak appointed him to be in charge of the White army in the region where his anti-Bolshevik army was supported by British forces. However, after an unsuccessful advance against the Red Army along the northern Dvina in the summer of 1919, British forces withdrew from the region and Miller's men faced the enemy alone, eventually being evacuated to Norway in February 1920.

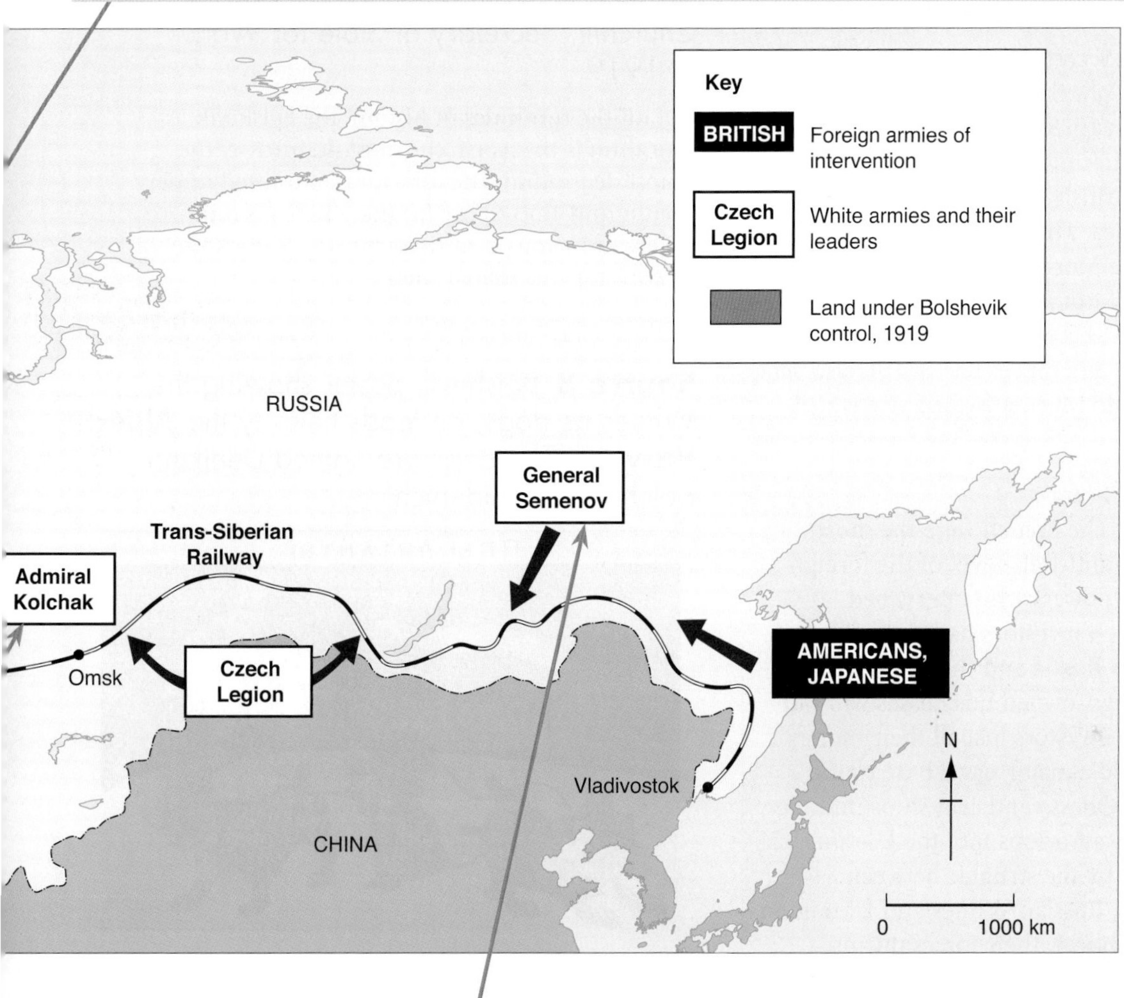


### White General Semenov in the east

Semenov commanded White forces in the Siberian region supported by Japanese forces. After the defeat of the White movement, Admiral Kolchak transferred power to Semenov in the Far East. However, Semenov was unable to keep his forces in Siberia under control: they stole, burned, murdered and raped civilians, and developed a reputation for being little better than thugs. In July 1920 the Japanese Expeditionary Corps started their withdrawal, leaving Semenov without support, and he was defeated by units of the Red Army in October 1920.

## TASKS

1 Describe what happened to Denikin's armies.
(For guidance on answering this type of question, see page 79.)

2 Using only the map, give the strengths and weaknesses of the Whites.

# What part was played by foreign powers in the Civil War?

**Britain**

Winston Churchill, the British Secretary of State for War, saw the Whites as crusaders against Bolshevism. In 1918 British forces entered Transcaucasia in southern Russia and also occupied part of central Asia. British warships sailed into the Baltic and the Black Sea. The British sent troops to occupy Archangel and Murmansk. The British called their contingent the North Russian Expeditionary Force (NREF) and it was comprised mostly of men not fit enough to serve in France. The British also sent two training missions to Murmansk and Archangel.

**France**

The French were the most anti-Bolshevik of the foreign powers who intervened in the Civil War. French investors had poured millions of francs into Russia and the Bolsheviks had nationalised foreign-owned businesses without compensation, so the investors lost all their money. The French established a major naval base round the Black Sea port of Odessa and sent ships into the Black Sea. They also sent troops into the Ukraine but became confused by the struggle between Russian Communists, Russian Whites and Ukrainian nationalists. They withdrew their forces during March and April 1919, having hardly fired a shot.

**Japan**

The Japanese saw the Civil War as a further opportunity for expansion and sent a sizeable force into Siberia, especially round Vladivostock and occupied other parts of Siberia.

**USA**

US involvement was partly due to the fear of the spread of communism but also to stop the Japanese from annexing land from Russia. They sent troops to Siberia and to Archangel.

**Source A** From a speech by Winston Churchill, Secretary of State for War, in 1919

*Of all the tyrannies in history, the Bolshevik tyranny is the worst, the most destructive, the most degrading. The atrocities committed under Lenin and Trotsky are far more hideous and more numerous that those for which the Kaiser of Germany was responsible.*

**Source B** Bolshevik poster showing the Whites as dogs, on leads held by the **Allied Powers**. The dogs are named Denikin, Kolchak and Yudenich

## TASKS

1 Use the information in Source A and your own knowledge to explain why the British supported the Whites during the Civil War. (For guidance on answering this type of question, see page 40.)

2 How successful were the actions of foreign powers during the Civil War? (For guidance on answering this type of question, see page 113.)

3 How useful is Source B to a historian studying foreign intervention in the Civil War? (For guidance on answering this type of question, see pages 59–60.)

# What was the role of Trotsky and the Red Army in the Civil War?

In contrast to the various armies and commanders that opposed the Bolsheviks, the Reds had one commander, Trotsky, and one army, the Red Army. As you can see on the map on pages 62–63, the Reds occupied central Russia and had command of the railways, which enabled them to move troops and supplies more easily than the Whites. They also controlled the two key cities of Petrograd and Moscow.

## Trotsky

Lenin realised that Trotsky was the only person that could save the revolution and appointed him as Commissar of War in March 1918. Trotsky's strengths were his energy, passion and organisational abilities. He restored discipline and professionalism to what he now called the 'Workers' and Peasants' Red Army' and turned it into an effective fighting force.

- Trotsky restored conscription in order to raise a large army of five million.
- He removed soldiers' committees and the election of officers, replacing them with a traditional officer structure.
- He brought back thousands of former tsarist officers who were unemployed and poor and wanted to get back to the job they knew. To ensure their loyalty, Trotsky had their families kept hostage.
- He promoted talented soldiers who had never made officers in the nobility-dominated tsarist army. These men, such as Tuchachevsky and Zhukov, became the Red Army's best generals.
- Trotsky appointed a Bolshevik political commissar to each army unit. The commissar kept an eye on the officers and ensured they were following the **party line**.
- He restored strict military discipline, bringing back the death penalty for a range of offences.

Trotsky was not a backroom commander who remained far behind enemy lines. Travelling in a specially equipped train, he rushed to the points where the fighting was it at its fiercest to provide support. His presence seemed to make a difference and inspire the troops. It was Trotsky who decided to save Petrograd when it was under threat from Yudenich (see page 62). The capital had been moved to Moscow and Lenin was prepared to sacrifice Petrograd. Trotsky disagreed and, in his special train, raced to the front where Yudenich's army was turned away.

**Source A** From a report by a British intelligence agent, 1918

*The position of officers of the old tsarist army in the Red Army is painful in the extreme. Mobilised for service but mistrusted, they are shot for the least failure of their troops. By a recent order of Trotsky's, the wives and children of officers who desert to the Whites are thrown into prison.*

**Source B** Trotsky on his special train visiting Red Army troops during the Civil War

**Source C** A description of the impact of a visit by Trotsky to the front during the Civil War. This was written by a member of the Red Army in 1920

*The town of Gomel was about to fall into the enemy's hands when Trotsky arrived. Then everything changed and the tide began to turn. Trotsky's arrival meant that the city would not be abandoned. He paid a visit to the front lines and made a speech. We were lifted by the energy he carried wherever a critical situation arose. The situation, which was catastrophic 24 hours earlier, had improved by his coming – as though by a miracle.*

## The Red Army

**Source D** A Bolshevik poster of 1919 which is praising the three million-strong Red Army

By the end of 1919 the Red Army had three million troops and around five million a year later. It was generally well supplied due to War Communism (see page 82), which meant that all necessary resources were poured into the army – even if this meant peasants and workers went hungry. However, it did have its weaknesses.

- Once the supply of town workers ran out, Trotsky conscripted peasants. Peasants were often reluctant conscripts who deserted during harvest time. It was estimated that nearly one million deserted in 1918, taking their weapons and equipment with them.
- Some peasants staged uprisings against conscription and many joined the independent Green armies.
- In the later stages of the war, the Red Army was often poorly equipped. Few had good boots and there was a shortage of ammunition. This is why Trotsky's train carried uniforms and supplies.
- There was frequent indiscipline. Some were full-scale mutinies during which officers were murdered and new officers elected.

### TASKS

1. How useful is Source A (on page 65) to a historian studying the Red Army during the Civil War? (For guidance on answering this type of question, see pages 59–60.)
2. How far does Source B (on page 65) support the view that Trotsky's leadership was important during the Civil War? (For guidance on answering this type of question, see pages 48–49.)
3. Use the information from Source C (on page 65) and your own knowledge to explain why Trotsky's leadership was important during the Civil War. (For guidance on answering this type of question, see page 40.)
4. What does Source D show about the Red Army? (For guidance on answering this type of question, see page 22.)
5. Working in pairs, produce a mind map that shows the changes which Trotsky brought to the Red Army. Rank these changes in order clockwise, beginning with the most important at 12 o'clock.

# What happened to the tsar and his family?

On 19 July 1918, a Bolshevik newspaper announced the death of Nicholas II and that the 'wife and son of Nicholas Romanov have been sent to a safe place'. In fact, all the royal family had been murdered but the Bolsheviks were afraid to acknowledge that they had killed the wife and children in case it lost them public sympathy and annoyed the Germans because Alexandra, the tsar's wife, was German.

## The tsar and his family 1917–18

After his abdication in February 1917, the tsar and his family were allowed to live in the royal palace at Tsarskoye Selo. However, this was close to Petrograd and the **Provisional Government** was afraid that the royal family was so unpopular that they would be attacked by local people. Therefore, they were moved to Tobolsk in Siberia.

As the White armies gained control of Siberia in April 1918, the family were moved again. The Bolsheviks sent them to Ekaterinburg in the Ural Mountains. They were met at the station by an angry mob and imprisoned in a large white house which had belonged to a retired businessman.

## Reasons for the murder

Right until the collapse of communism in Russia in the late twentieth century, the Soviet authorities insisted that the murder was carried out by the local Bolsheviks in Ekaterinburg who feared that the Romanovs would fall into the hands of the advancing White armies.

The opening up of the Soviet archives in the 1990s showed that, in fact, the decision was taken by Lenin in the first week of July 1918 because of advice given to him by Goloshchekin, a leading Bolshevik. Goloshchekin was sent to Ekaterinburg to organise the execution and sent a coded telegram to Lenin on 16 July informing him that the execution had to take place because the Czech Legion was surrounding the city. The local Bolsheviks had only a few hundred Red Guards and little chance of safely evacuating the Romanovs. There was every chance that the royal family would be handed over to the Whites and provide an even greater focal point for the opponents of the Bolsheviks. Indeed, the city fell to the Czechs eight days after the murder.

**Source A** From an entry in Trotsky's diary of 1935 in which he recalls a conversation with Sverdlov, a leading Bolshevik, shortly after the murder

*Speaking with Sverdlov, I asked in passing, 'Oh, yes, where is the tsar?' 'Finished', he replied. 'He has been shot'. 'And where is the family?' 'The family has been shot along with him'. 'All?', I asked. 'All', Sverdlov replied. 'And who decided the matter?', I enquired. 'We decided it here. Illich [Lenin] thought that we should not leave the Whites a live banner, especially under the present difficult circumstances'.*

**TASK**

1 Explain why the tsar and his family were murdered in 1918.
(For guidance on answering this type of question, see page 90.)

2 How far does Source A support the view that the Bolshevik leaders made the decision to execute the tsar and his family?
(For guidance on answering this type of question, see pages 48–49.)

## The murder

On 4 July the local *Cheka*, led by Yakov Yurovsky, took over the responsibility of guarding the Romanovs and carrying out the execution. At 2a.m. on 17 July, Nicholas and his family were led into the basement of the house. None of them seemed aware of what was about to happen. They had been told that there had been shooting in the street and it was safer for them to be in the basement.

Yurovsky entered the room with the murder squad – six Hungarians. He read out the order to shoot the Romanovs. Nicholas asked him to repeat and his last words were 'What? What?' Yurovsky shot Nicholas at point blank range. Nicholas and his wife died instantly. Despite firing many shots, Alexis and Anastasia still showed signs of life. Alexis was finished off by two shots from Yurovsky and Anastasia was bayoneted several times.

After the murder, the bodies were dumped in a nearby mineshaft. This turned out to be too shallow to conceal the bodies and, the following day, the bodies were driven off in a lorry and buried in the ground. Sulphuric acid was poured on their faces to hide the identity of the corpses should they be discovered. News of the execution reached Lenin the following day. The real significance of the murder was that it was a declaration of terror. It was a statement that from now on individuals would count for nothing in the Civil War.

### TASKS

**3** How useful is Source B to a historian studying the murder of the Romanovs? (For guidance on answering this type of question, see pages 59–60.)

**4** Put together a newspaper headline for the Whites to go with the painting of the assassination of the Romanovs.

**Source B** A painting by Sarmet, a White supporter, showing the murder of the Romanovs. It was painted in 1923 and based on a White investigation into the assassination

# Examination guidance

This section provides guidance on how to answer a historical interpretation through the analysis, evaluation and cross-referencing of two sources question. This is worth 8 marks.

Why do Sources A and B have different views about the involvement of foreign powers in the Civil War? In your answer you should refer to both the content of the sources and the authors. (8 marks)

There is a candidate response to this question on page 70.

These sources say different things about the involvement of foreign powers in the Civil War.

**Source A** A Bolshevik propaganda poster issued in 1919. It shows France, America and Britain as evil capitalists who are trying to take control of Russia

## Tips on how to answer

- You need to refer to the content of both sources, relate this to your own knowledge of this period and consider the attribution of both sources. This will require you to perform a thorough COP (content, origin, purpose) evaluation of both sources.
- You need to read through both sources with care, underlining or highlighting the most important details. You can also scribble some notes in the margin around the source about how it fits into your knowledge of this period
  - Does it confirm what you know?
  - Does it only refer to part of the answer and are some important points missing?
  - Does it agree or disagree with what is said in the other source?
- This will enable you to compare and contrast the two sources in terms of their content value.
- You now need to consider the origin of each source, saying who the authors are and when they made these observations. Are they primary or secondary sources, for example?
- You should then consider the purpose of each source, noting the circumstances under which they were written. For example, is the source written by a modern historian or a contemporary? Does the author display a biased point of view and if so, why?
- To obtain maximum marks, you need to produce a balanced answer with good support from both sources and your own knowledge, together with a detailed consideration of the attributions of each source.

**Source B** Part of a speech made by Winston Churchill in 1919 when he was the British Secretary for War

*There is an allied army in occupation of considerable regions of north Russia ... They <u>were sent there as part of our operations against Germany</u>. It was vitally necessary to take every measure in regard to Russia during the war which would <u>keep as many German troops as possible on the Russian front</u>, and <u>prevent the movement of German armies to the Western front</u> ... <u>That is the reason why we gave aid to the armies of Admiral Kolchak and General Denikin</u>.*

Underlinings made by the candidate during the exam.

## Response by candidate

*Sources A and B have very different views about the involvement of foreign powers in the Civil War because they were produced by opposite sides in the war. Source A is a Bolshevik propaganda poster issued in 1919. It shows France, America and Britain as evil capitalists who are trying to take control of the poor Russian people. The foreign powers are portrayed as being fat and greedy. They display no interest in looking after the Russian people who are made to look weak and starved under a greedy capitalist system. The purpose of the source was to generate hatred inside Russia for the foreign powers and to encourage support for the Bolsheviks. The Bolsheviks wanted to be seen as the saviours of Russia against the evil forces of the Whites who were really controlled by the big powers like America, France and Britain.*

Considers the **origin** of Source A and examines its **content** and **purpose**.

*The message of Source A contrasts sharply with that of Source B which is part of a speech delivered by Winston Churchill in 1919. Like Source A it is a primary source, dating from the same year, 1919. Churchill is saying that the only reason the allied armies are fighting in Russia is to continue the war against Germany. The allies needed Russia to stay in the war to force Germany to fight on two fronts, the Eastern and Western Fronts. That is said to be the reason why the allies sent forces to help the White commanders Admiral Kolchak and General Denikin. As the Secretary of War, Churchill has to justify the reasons for British intervention but in his speech he does not spell out the full reasons for this intervention. Britain, France and America were also keen to stop the spread of communism outside Russia. They disliked the Bolsheviks and wanted to see them fall from power. Churchill is not therefore giving the full picture.*

Considers the **origin** of Source B and examines its **content** and **purpose**.

*The two sources say opposite things because of the circumstances under which they were written. Both are pieces of propaganda. Source A is trying to paint the foreign powers as being greedy capitalists who want to control Russia. Source B is trying to say that the foreign powers are only involved to keep Russia in the war against Germany. Both are very narrow in their focus and do not give the full picture. The main reason why they say different things about the involvement of foreign powers is because one is produced by supporters of the Reds and the other by supporters of the Whites and they each want to downplay the other side and justify their standpoint.*

Compares the reliability of both sources. Concludes with a link back to the question.

### Examiner's comment

This is a well-developed answer. The candidate has performed a thorough evaluation of each source, with clear reference to content, origin and purpose. The content has been explained and put into context, linking the material to the bigger picture. There is a good consideration of both attributions, referring to the origin and purpose of each source, spelling out the reasons for possible bias and/or reliability issues. The concluding paragraph compares and contrasts both sources and ends with a direct link back to the question. The answer reaches the highest level and is worthy of receiving the maximum of 8 marks.

# Why were the Reds able to win the Civil War?

The Bolshevik victory in the Civil War was due to their own strengths as well as the weaknesses of the opposition, the Whites. The Reds benefited from strong and unified leadership under Lenin and Trotsky as well as their geographical location, controlling the central area round Moscow and Petrograd. On the other hand, the Whites suffered from divisions between their leaders and were scattered on the edges of Russia, which made communication very difficult.

This chapter answers the following questions:

- What were the strengths of the Reds?
- What were the weaknesses of the Whites?

**Source A** A Red propaganda leaflet of 1918 targeting foreign troops. It had the title 'Why Have You Come to Murmansk?'

*For the first time in history the working people have got control of their country. The workers of all countries are striving to achieve this objective. We in Russia have succeeded. We have thrown off the rule of the tsar and of capitalists. But we still have tremendous difficulties to overcome. We cannot build a new society in a day. We ask you, are you going to crush us? To help give Russia back to the landlords, the capitalists and the tsar?*

Examination guidance

Throughout this chapter you will be given the opportunity to practise different exam-style questions and detailed guidance on how to answer a 'describe' question. This is worth 5 marks.

**TASK**

What can you learn from Source A about Bolshevik propaganda during the Civil War?

# What were the strengths of the Reds?

The main strengths of the Reds were the leadership of Lenin and Trotsky, their control of the railways, widespread support from the peasants through propaganda and their controversial policies of War Communism and terror.

## The leadership of Lenin and Trotsky

The Bolsheviks benefited from the centralised and unified leadership of Lenin and Trotsky. Lenin was the inspirational figure who provided the central political leadership and direction. He was also extremely ruthless in conducting the war, as shown by the introduction of War Communism and the use of the *Cheka* (see page 76). Severe discipline was enforced in factories and strict food rationing was introduced, with the largest rations going to the Red Army.

Trotsky was also key to the success of the Reds. He was able to inspire and rally men. As well as setting up and organising the Red Army, Trotsky decided the overall strategy of the Bolsheviks. This was to defend the Red Army's internal lines of communication and to deny the Whites the opportunity to concentrate large forces in one location. Bolshevik control of the railways was the key to this strategy. Most of the decisive battles between the Whites and Reds took place near railheads and depots.

**Source A** Trotsky, writing in his memoirs in 1930, about the setting up of the Red Army

*We were constructing an army all over again and under fire at that ... What was needed for this? It needed good commanders – a few dozen experienced fighters, a dozen or so Communists ready to make any sacrifice; boots for bare-footed, a bath house, propaganda, food, underwear, tobacco and matches.*

## Control of the central area and railways

As you can see from the map on page 62, the Reds occupied the central Russian-speaking area of the country, which made the territory easier to control and ensured that they had to travel shorter distances.

- They moved their capital to Moscow, at the hub of the railway network. The Reds made better use of the railway network than the Whites to transport men and munitions to the battlefronts. Railways were also of great importance in communications in Russia due to the poor state of most of the roads as well as the huge distances often involved in transporting troops and supplies.
- Most of the population lived in the central areas, which made it easier to conscript more people into the army as they needed. Red armies often vastly outnumbered their White opponents.
- This area also contained the main armaments factories in Russia, so the Bolsheviks could carry on producing war materials. Raw materials and finished goods could be moved more easily by trains. The stores of the tsarist army and the tsar's old **arsenals**, which contained 2.2 million rifles, 12,000 field guns and a great deal of ammunition, fell into their hands.

**Source B** A photograph of a Bolshevik armoured train in 1919

## Support from the peasantry

The support of the peasants was crucial since they supplied the main body of soldiers for both sides. They had little love for either side but were often more inclined to support the Bolsheviks because:

- Lenin had introduced the Decree of Land in 1917 (see page 54), which gave the peasants the right to the land, whereas the Whites made it clear that they would restore the land to its former owners. The White Admiral Kolchak even gave estates to landlords who had not owned them before the revolution.

- The brutality of the White armies drove many peasants to support the Bolsheviks as the lesser of two evils. For example, the Cossacks in the southern White army practised 'ethnic cleansing', driving out thousands of non-Cossack peasants, especially Russians and Ukrainians, from their lands and treating them brutally.

## Propaganda and a cause

One of the most important factors explaining the success of the Reds was their driving sense of purpose. They were fighting for a cause, the preservation of the October Revolution, and this, together with the leadership of Lenin and Trotsky, often resulted in much higher morale and dedication in the Red Army compared to that of their opponents.

In addition, the Bolsheviks made very effective use of propaganda, using imaginative and powerful images and messages including:

- the Whites would take away land from the peasants
- foreign invaders were supporting the Whites and would control Russia (see propaganda poster on page 69)
- the Reds offered a wonderful new society for workers and peasants.

**Source C** From a report by Robert Bruce Lockhart, a British agent in Russia during the Civil War, November 1918

*It must be admitted that the success of Bolshevism in Russia is due to more deep-rooted causes than the terrorism of a band of workmen. The Bolshevik supporters may not number more than ten per cent of the population but their worst enemies cannot deny their energy and party discipline ... Some 70 per cent of the population – the majority of the peasantry – remain inactive. This inactivity is an advantage to the Bolsheviks whose influence among the peasantry is almost entirely the result of the Brest-Litovsk Treaty and the land issue.*

**Source D** A Bolshevik cartoon of 1919 showing General Denikin, a leading White commander, with the symbols of his terrorism in the background

## TASKS

1. How important was the leadership of Trotsky in securing Bolshevik victory in the Civil War? (For guidance on answering this type of question, see page 113.)
2. How far does Source A support the view that Trotsky was important during the Civil War? (For guidance on answering this type of question, see pages 48–49.)
3. What does Source B show you about the Bolshevik use of railways? (For guidance on answering this type of question, see page 22.)
4. Explain why control of the central area of Russia was important to the Reds during the Civil War. (For guidance on answering this type of question, see page 90.)
5. Explain why the majority of peasants supported the Reds during the Civil War. (For guidance on answering this type of question, see page 90.)
6. How far does Source D support the view that the Bolsheviks made effective use of propaganda during the Civil War? (For guidance on answering this type of question, see pages 48–49.)
7. How useful is Source C to a historian studying support for the Reds during the Civil War? (For guidance on answering this type of question, see pages 59–60.)

## War Communism

In 1918 Lenin introduced War Communism for several reasons as shown in the table below.

| Economic | Social | Political | Military |
|---|---|---|---|
| The peasants wanted to keep the land they had been given but were unwilling to sell the food they grew. Lenin wanted to control the supply of food for the towns. Prices had risen rapidly and there was inflation | There were severe shortages of food and other basic necessities in Russia | The policy followed the Communist idea of central control and direction of the economy | The Bolsheviks had to guarantee supplies for the huge Red Army during the Civil War against the Whites |

Lenin set up the Supreme Council of National Economy (***Vesenkha***) to create a planned economy and a fair society. By the middle of 1918, War Communism meant that the government controlled every aspect of economic life.

The main features of War Communism were:

- Rationing of food in cities was to be strictly applied during food shortages.
- Private trading was banned. Peasants could no longer sell their surplus food for profit but had to give it to the government. Lenin ordered squads into the countryside to seize food if peasants proved unwilling to surrender their produce. This was known as **food requisitioning**.
- Factories with more than ten workers were nationalised. This meant that the state now owned the factories. *Vesenkha* decided how much was to be produced in each industry. Workers were under government control and could be told where to work.
- Rapid inflation, which left money valueless. People had to barter, which meant exchanging goods rather than using money.

In theory, Lenin's decision to introduce War Communism was sound, but practically it was flawed. Both workers and peasants objected to it. When Lenin sent armed Bolsheviks into the countryside to confiscate their food, the peasants resisted fiercely. Lenin's answer to this was to turn other peasants against those who refused to hand over their grain. He called these peasants ***kulaks***, which means tight-fisted.

These policies encouraged opposition to the Bolsheviks, especially as it was very difficult to tell the difference between a *kulak* and an ordinary peasant. A group called Workers' Opposition was formed to press for changes to the policy. One of the group's calls was for 'Soviets without Communists'. Lenin's original land decrees (see page 54) had won the Bolsheviks support from the peasants. War Communism lost much of this support. The Bolsheviks even took the grain needed for sowing for the next crop. The result was a terrible famine in 1920–21.

It was vital that the Red Army was supplied with the weapons and food which it needed to fight the war effectively. War Communism was very effective in keeping the army supplied, but it led to widespread starvation among the peasants and workers of Russia.

**Source E** A White Russian poster of 1919, depicting food requisitioning

**Source F** From *Memoirs of a Revolutionary* by Victor Serge, 1945. Serge became a Bolshevik in 1919 but was expelled from the party in 1928. Here he is writing about food requisitioning

*Groups which were sent into the countryside to obtain grain by requisition might be driven away by the peasants with pitchforks. Savage peasants would slit open a Commissar's belly, pack it with grain, and leave him by the roadside as a lesson to all.*

**Source G** From a speech by Lenin to workers in Petrograd in August 1918

*These bloodsuckers have grown rich during the war on the people's want ... These spiders have grown fat at the expense of the peasants ... These leeches have drunk the blood of workers. Growing richer the more the workers starved in the cities and factories ... Merciless war against these* ***kulaks****. Death to them.*

**Source H** A Bolshevik poster of 1919 to encourage the requisition squads used to seize food in the countryside. The poster reads: 'You shed your blood for the workers' and peasants' revolution. The workers and peasants will deny themselves and give you their last clothes and boots. Take them!'

## TASKS

**8** Explain why the Bolsheviks introduced a policy of War Communism.
(For guidance on answering this type of question, see page 90.)

**9** How far does Source E support the view that War Communism was unpopular?
(For guidance on answering this type of question, see pages 48–49.)

**10** What does Source F tell you about reactions to War Communism?

**11** How useful is Source H to a historian studying War Communism during the Civil War?
(For guidance on answering this type of question, see pages 59–60.)

**12** Why do Sources E and G have different views about War Communism?
(For guidance on answering this type of question, see pages 69–70.)

## The use of the *Cheka*

Another important contribution to the Bolshevik victory was the *Cheka* or secret police (see page 94). This organisation was responsible for dealing with law and order and political opposition to the Bolsheviks. In 1918 its leader, Felix Dzerhinsky, began the 'Red Terror' in which those suspected of working against the revolution were arrested, tortured and executed.

The *Cheka* stepped up its campaign after an unsuccessful attempt to assassinate Lenin in August 1918. In Petrograd alone over 800 so-called 'enemies of the state' were executed. By the end of the Civil War, an estimated 200,000 had been killed and a further 85,000 put in prison by the secret police.

There were numerous rumours about the cruelty of the *Cheka*:

- In Kharkov, Chekists scalped their prisoners and took their skin off their hands like gloves.
- In Voronezh they placed naked prisoners in a barrel punctured with nails and then set it in motion.
- In Tsaritsyn and Kamyyshin they severed bones with a saw.
- In Poltava they impaled 18 monks and burned at the stake peasants who had rebelled.

**Source I** The *Cheka*'s orders to the soviets, February 1918, published in *Pravda*

*The All-Russian Extraordinary Commission for the Struggle Against Counter-Revolution, Sabotage and Speculation asks the local soviets to proceed at once to seek out, arrest and shoot immediately all members connected with counter-revolutionary organisations. (1) agents of enemy spies, (2) counter-revolutionary agitators, (3) organisers of revolts against the Soviet government, (4) buyers and sellers of arms to be used by the counter-revolutionary bourgeoisie – all these to be shot on the spot when caught red-handed in the act.*

### TASKS

**13** Describe how the Bolsheviks used the *Cheka* during the Civil War.
(For guidance on answering this type of question, see page 79.)

**14** How useful is Source I to a historian studying the use of the *Cheka* during the Civil War?
(For guidance on answering this type of question, see pages 59–60.)

**15** In pairs, put together a mind map summarising the strengths of the Reds during the Civil War. On your mind map draw lines showing links between any of these factors. On the line briefly explain these links.

**16** How important were the different strengths of the Reds in helping them to win the Civil War? Make a copy of the following grid and give each reason a rating of 1–5, with 5 being the highest. Briefly explain each decision.

| Reason | Rating | Brief explanation |
|---|---|---|
| Leadership | | |
| Central area | | |
| Peasantry | | |
| Propaganda | | |
| War Communism | | |
| *Cheka* | | |

# What were the weaknesses of the Whites?

The success of the Reds in the Civil War was greatly assisted by the weaknesses of their opponents.

## Lack of unity

Whereas the Bolsheviks were one political party with a single leadership, the Whites were made up of many different political parties who constantly squabbled and did not trust each other.

- They could not agree on whether they were fighting for **monarchism** or **republicanism** or for the Constituent Assembly. This made it hard for them to co-operate and impossible to develop a common political aim.
- They had little chance of developing a co-ordinated military strategy. Often the White generals would not work together because they did not like or trust each other. For example, other generals were suspicious of Kolchak's motives and intentions. This played right into the hands of Trotsky who was able to deal with each of the White armies in turn, rather than mounting a joint, simultaneous attack on all fronts.

## Geographical spread

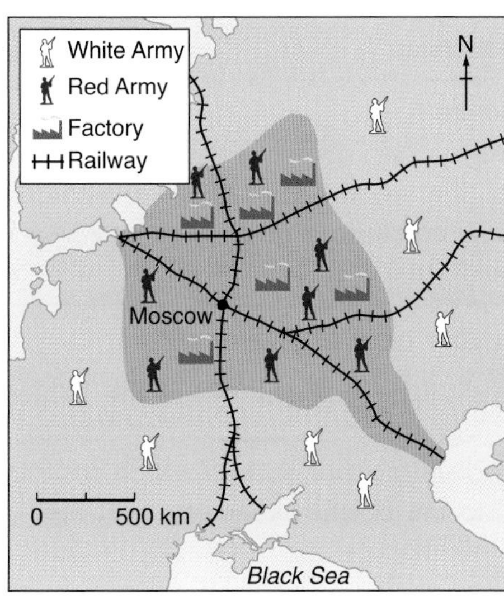


The Whites were scattered round the edges of the central area, separated by large distances, as shown in the map above.

- This made communications difficult, especially moving men and weapons. They had to use officers on horseback to convey messages.
- It was very difficult to co-ordinate the attacks of the various White armies.
- The central area, controlled by the Bolsheviks, was heavily populated. Many of the areas under White control were thinly populated, which made it difficult to conscript large armies.
- They did not control the railways and often had to transport troops and supplies across huge distances using very poor roads.

## Nationalist groups

The Whites lost the support of nationalist groups. White leaders wanted to restore the Russian Empire with its pre-1917 borders. This antagonised **separatists** such as the Ukrainians and Georgians who were looking for greater self-government, if not independence.

## Weak support from foreign powers

Foreign support should have worked in the favour of the Whites. It certainly brought them supplies and weapons. However, it was half-hearted and ineffective.

- There was lukewarm support from most of the British government and the British public.
- French soldiers were not keen to fight and there were mutinies in the French fleet in the Black Sea.
- The Japanese were more interested in trying to acquire some valuable territory than in fighting the Bolsheviks.
- Foreign involvement gave the Bolsheviks a major propaganda opportunity. They could present themselves as the defenders of Russian soil against foreign forces.

### TASKS

1. Explain why the White forces were not united. (For guidance on answering this type of question, see page 90.)
2. Explain why the Whites were weakened by their geographical spread. (For guidance on answering this type of question, see page 90.)

## Poor leadership

The Whites, for the most part, had poor leaders. No White leader of the stature of Trotsky or Lenin emerged.

- Several were cruel and treated their men with contempt much the same as the treatment during the tsarist regime. Therefore, there was little loyalty from the soldiers, many of whom deserted.
- There were very high levels of corruption and indiscipline in the White armies. For example, in Omsk, which was where Kolchak was based, uniforms and munitions, supplied by foreign allies, were sold on the black market. Officers lived in brothels and were often under the influence of cocaine and/or vodka.
- The Whites were never more than an uncoordinated collection of separate forces whose morale was never high.
- The White generals could not agree on strategy. They were responsible for much brutality.

**Source A** From the diary of Colonel Drozdovsky, May 1919. He was a White commander during the Civil War

*Having surrounded the village, the Whites fired a couple of volleys in the direction of the village and everyone took cover. Then the mounted soldiers entered the village, met the Bolshevik committee and put the members to death. After the execution, the houses of the culprits were burned and the male population under 45 was whipped. Then the population was ordered to deliver without pay the best cattle, pigs, fowl and bread for the soldiers as well as the best horses.*

**Source B** A sketch made by a Bolshevik artist during the Civil War. It shows Denikin's troops executing Bolsheviks

## TASKS

**3** Use the information in Source A and your own knowledge to explain why the Whites lost much support during the Civil War.
(For guidance on answering this type of question, see page 40.)

**4** How useful is Source B to a historian studying the activities of the Whites during the Civil War?
(For guidance on answering this type of question, see pages 59–60.)

**5** Working in pairs, put together a mind map showing the main weaknesses of the Whites during the Civil War. Rank these in order of importance clockwise, beginning with the most important at 12 o'clock.

**6** Make a copy of and complete the following grid comparing the Reds and Whites during the Civil War.

| Factors | Reds | Whites |
|---|---|---|
| Unity | | |
| Geographical location | | |
| Support | | |
| Leadership | | |
| Morale | | |

**7** Was the weakness of the White forces the main reason for the Bolshevik victory in the Civil War?

In your answer you should:
- discuss the weakness of the White forces
- discuss other factors which contributed to the Bolshevik victory over the Whites.

(For guidance on answering this type of question, see pages 101–2.)

# Examination guidance

This section provides guidance on how to answer a 'describe' question. This is worth 4 marks.

Describe the policy of War Communism. **(4 marks)**

### Response by candidate

*The policy of War Communism was introduced by Lenin in mid-1918 to enforce state control over agricultural and industrial production. Its aim was to keep the Red Army supplied with food and weapons during the Civil War and it remained in operation until 1921. In the towns the state took control of industry and told factories what to produce. There was strict discipline of the workers who were forbidden to leave the cities. Strikes were made illegal. Food was rationed and only given to those in work.*

*In the countryside peasants were forced to hand over surplus food supplies. The Cheka were used to requisition food and peasants who resisted were harshly treated. The actions of the Cheka became very brutal and resulted in the Red Terror. By 1921 the economy was in ruins. Industrial output had fallen under War Communism and agriculture had collapsed. Farmers grew less and the shortage of food led to a terrible famine. In 1921 Lenin was forced to abandon the policy of War Communism.*

A range of key factors are identified and discussed in some detail.

Specific factual detail is included throughout the answer.

## Tips on how to answer

- Make sure you only include information that is directly relevant.
- It is a good idea to start your answer using the words from the question. For example, 'The policy of War Communism was …'.
- Try to include specific factual details such as dates, events, the names of key people. The more informed your description the higher the mark you will receive.
- Aim to cover at least two key points.

### Examiner's comment

The candidate has produced a detailed answer which covers a range of factors such as when and why the policy of War Communism was introduced, how it operated in the cities and countryside, the work of the requisition squads and the harshness of the policy. The **range and depth of detail** places the response at the highest level, allowing it to score the maximum of 4 marks.

### Now you have a go

Describe Trotsky's leadership of the Red Army during the Civil War. **(4 marks)**

This section examines the key features of the Communist state in the years 1921–24. During these years, Lenin introduced major changes in his economic policies, from **War Communism**, which was very unpopular in the cities and the countryside, to the **New Economic Policy** (**NEP**) that had some definite features of capitalism. Moreover, Lenin used various methods to establish a Communist state in Russia including the ***Cheka*** and **Red Terror** and government control of propaganda and censorship. Lenin's death in 1924 was followed by a leadership struggle, mainly between the favourite, Trotsky, and the outsider, Stalin. There are mixed interpretations of Lenin's achievements in Russia. His death was followed by the 'Lenin cult', a period of hero worship in the **USSR**. However, his critics argue that he paved the way for the horrors of Stalin's era.

Each chapter explains a key issue and examines important lines of enquiry as outlined below:

**Chapter 7**: Why did Lenin introduce the New Economic Policy and how successful was it?

- Why did Lenin introduce the New Economic Policy?
- What were the main features of the New Economic Policy?
- How successful was the New Economic Policy?

**Chapter 8**: Did Lenin succeed in establishing a Communist state in Russia?

- How did Lenin create the organs of the Communist state?
- How did centralisation increase under Lenin's leadership?
- What was life like under Communist rule?

**Source A** From a speech by Lenin in which he justifies the introduction of the New Economic Policy

*The civil war of 1918–20 greatly increased the devastation of the country, retarded the restoration of its means of production, and bled the* ***proletariat*** *more than any other class. To this was added the failure of the harvest of 1920, the fodder shortage, the dying off of cattle, which still further retarded the restoration of transport and industry, because, among other things, it interfered with the employment of peasants' horses for carting wood, our main fuel.*

**TASK**

What does Source A tell you about the problems of Russia in 1921?

**Chapter 9**: What was Lenin's legacy to Russia?

- Why was there a power struggle to succeed Lenin?
- Who were the leadership rivals?
- How did the rivals struggle for power?
- Why was Stalin favourite to succeed Lenin by the end of 1924?
- What was Lenin's legacy to Russia?

# 7 Why did Lenin introduce the New Economic Policy and how successful was it?

Within months of seizing power, Lenin introduced War Communism as a method of controlling the economy as well as supplying the needs of the Red Army during the Civil War. This proved extremely unpopular with the peasants and industrial workers and seriously undermined the popularity of the **Bolshevik** regime. This dissatisfaction was shown by the Kronstadt Mutiny of 1921 which prompted the end of War Communism, to be replaced by the New Economic Policy (NEP). The NEP included elements of capitalism which upset some of the Bolshevik Party faithful.

This chapter answers the following questions:

- Why did Lenin introduce the NEP?
- What were the main features of the NEP?
- How successful was the NEP?

### Examination guidance

Throughout this chapter you will be given the opportunity to practise different exam-style questions and detailed guidance on how to answer an 'explain' question. This is worth 5 marks.

**Source A** Nikolai Izachik, a Bolshevik Party member, recalling in the 1980s the introduction of the New Economic Policy (NEP) in 1921

*In 1921 we used to discuss the NEP for hours on end at Communist Party meetings. Most people supported Lenin. Others thought he was wrong. Many even tore up their Communist Party cards.*

### TASK

What can you learn from Source A about reactions to the NEP?

# Why did Lenin introduce the New Economic Policy?

Lenin introduced the New Economic Policy (NEP) because of the desperate situation in Russia at the end of the Civil War, the unpopularity of War Communism and growing opposition to the Communist government as shown by the Kronstadt Mutiny.

## The effects of War Communism

War Communism was brought in by Lenin to provide for the economic needs of the Red Army during the Civil War (see page 74). War Communism was successful on one level because it supplied the Red Army with food and enabled the victory over the Whites. However, the policy failed to create the **utopian Communist state** Lenin hoped for. Peasants did not respond to the idea of giving up produce to the state, and so they grew less grain and bred fewer animals. The resulting food shortage in 1920 developed into a famine in 1921. It has been estimated that about seven million people died during the famine. There had to be international aid for Russia in the crisis.

**Source A** Industrial and agricultural output in Russia comparing 1913 with 1921

| Output (millions of tonnes) | 1913 | 1921 |
|---|---|---|
| Grain | 80 | 37.6 |
| Sugar | 1.3 | 0.05 |
| Coal | 29 | 9 |
| Iron | 4.2 | 0.1 |
| Steel | 4.3 | 0.2 |
| Oil | 9.2 | 3.8 |
| Electricity (in millions of kWh) | 2039 | 520 |

**Source B** Starving Russian peasants trading in human flesh during the Civil War

**Source C** Children starving during the Civil War

## Growing opposition in the countryside

The main threat to the new Communist government came from the peasants in the countryside. They were discontented due to grain requisitioning which continued after the Civil War in order to provide food for the cities. According to *Cheka* sources, in February 1921, there were 118 separate uprisings throughout Russia. The most serious revolt was in the Tambov region where, for almost a year, the Red Army was unable to deal with a peasant army led by Alexander Antonov. At the height of the rebellion, large parts of the Tambov region were no-go areas for the Communist authorities.

## Growing opposition in the cities

The workers in the cities were also discontented because:

- They were forced to work long hours under strict new laws that included the death penalty for striking.
- Their rations were completely inadequate and often there were no rations at all.
- Some peasants brought food to barter or sell in the cities, but the price of this **black market** food was too high for most workers. Those caught trading for profit were often shot.

The big cities soon began to empty as workers returned to the countryside in the hope of finding food. Petrograd lost 70 per cent of its inhabitants and Moscow lost 50 per cent during the years of War Communism.

## Growing unrest

Many of those who remained in the cities became more and more opposed to the government. Even more serious for Lenin, there was opposition from within the Communist Party. A group called Workers' Opposition was formed to press for changes to the policy. They argued that War Communism was wrong and that the Communists should do more for the working classes. One of the group's calls was for '**Soviets** without Communists'.

In the cities, the severe winter of 1920–21 brought repeated strikes. In January 1921, the bread ration was cut by one-third in several cities, including Moscow and Petrograd. Food demonstrations had to be broken up by the *Cheka* and special troops because ordinary soldiers refused to fire on the crowds. The political **commissars** sent by Lenin to negotiate were ignored by the strikers.

**Source D** From *My Disillusionment in Russia, 1923*. This was written by a US woman, E. Goldman, who returned to Petrograd in 1920. She had lived in Russia in the 1880s but then returned to the USA

*It was almost in ruins, as if a hurricane had swept over it. The streets were dirty and deserted. All life had gone from them. The people walked about like living corpses. The shortage of food and fuel was slowly sapping the city. Grim death was clutching at its heart. Emaciated and frostbitten men, women and children were being whipped by a common lash, the search for a piece of bread or a stick of wood. It was a heart-rending sight by day, an oppressing weight by night. It fairly haunted me, this oppressive silence broken only by the occasional shots.*

## TASKS

1. What does Source B tell you about the effects of War Communism?
   (For guidance on answering this type of question, see page 22.)
2. Work in pairs. You live in Russia in 1920 and are an opponent of War Communism.
   - Using evidence from Sources A, B and C write a letter to *Pravda* criticising the policy.
   - Write a reply to be published in *Pravda* on behalf of the Bolshevik government.
3. Explain why there was growing opposition in the cities to the Bolsheviks.
   (For guidance on answering this type of question, see page 90.)
4. How far does Source D support the view that the situation in Russian cities was desperate? (For guidance on answering this type of question, see pages 48–49.)
5. How useful is Source A to a historian studying the impact of War Communism?
   (For guidance on answering this type of question, see pages 59–60.)

**Source E** From a speech by Petrechenko, a spokesman for the demonstrators, to the commissars at a public meeting, February 1921

*You are comfortable, you are warm. You commissars live in the palaces. Comrades, look around you and you will see that we have fallen into a terrible mire. We were pulled into this mire by a group of Communist bureaucrats who, under the mask of communism, have feathered their own nests in our republic. I myself was a Communist, and I call on you, comrades, drive out these false Communists who set worker against peasant and peasant against worker. Enough shooting of our brothers!*

## The Kronstadt Mutiny

In March 1921, there was a rebellion of sailors at the naval base of Kronstadt against the Bolshevik government. This was the greatest challenge for Lenin and Trotsky over War Communism. Thousands of sailors protested at events in Russia and objected, like the Workers' Opposition, to the way the Communist Party (the Bolsheviks were now called Communists) was taking power away from the soviets.

**Source F** A painting showing a meeting of sailors during the Kronstadt Mutiny, March 1921. Extracts from the meeting are shown in the speech bubbles

**Source G** What the Kronstadt sailors demanded

- *Because the present soviets do not express the will of the workers and peasants, new elections should be held.*
- *Freedom of speech and press to be granted to workers and peasants.*
- *Freedom of assembly and of trade unions and peasants' associations.*
- *All political prisoners belonging to Socialist parties to be set free.*

## The reaction of the Communist government

Lenin wanted no opposition and decided to stop the protests. The demands of the protestors came as a shock to him, especially as the Kronstadt sailors had proved to be some of his most loyal supporters. Trotsky had to use the Red Army to put down the rebellion. He ordered General Tukhachevsky to attack the naval base using 60,000 troops. During a three-week struggle over 20,000 men were killed or wounded in the fighting. The surviving rebels were either executed by the *Cheka* or put in a ***gulag***. For other opponents, the end of the rebellion meant the end of any hope of removing the Communists.

Lenin realised he had to change the policy – for him, Kronstadt was the 'flash that lit up reality'. In March 1921, Lenin abandoned War Communism and introduced the New Economic Policy in its place.

**Source H** From a report to Trotsky by the army commander, Tukhachevsky, after the defeat of the sailors

*The sailors fought like wild beasts. I cannot understand where they found the might for such rage. An entire company fought for an hour to capture one house and when the house was captured it was found to contain two or three soldiers at a machine gun. They seemed half dead but they snatched their revolvers and gasped, 'We didn't shoot enough of you bastards'.*

**Source I** From a report by Lenin to the Tenth Congress of the Russian Communist Party, a day after the Red Army forces began operations to suppress the Kronstadt uprising, 8 March 1921

*It shows what I said in dealing with our platforms discussion: in face of this danger we must understand that we must do more than put an end to party disputes as a matter of form – we shall do that, of course. We need to remember that we must take a much more serious approach to this question. We have to understand that, with the peasant economy in the grip of a crisis, we can survive only by appealing to the peasants to help town and countryside. The political danger here is obvious. A number of revolutions have clearly gone that way; we have always been mindful of this possibility and have warned against it.*

## TASKS

**6** How useful is Source F to a historian studying opposition to the Communist government?
(For guidance on answering this type of question, see pages 59–60.)

**7** Work in pairs to produce a reply by the commissars to Sources E and G.

**8** Use the information in Source G and your own knowledge to explain why there was an uprising at Kronstadt.
(For guidance on answering this type of question, see page 40.)

**9** Produce a newspaper headline for *Pravda*, the official government newspaper, about the rebellion.

**10** How useful is Source H to a historian studying the Kronstadt Rebellion?
(For guidance on answering this type of question, see pages 59–60.)

**11** How far does Source I support the view that the Kronstadt Rebellion encouraged Lenin to bring in change?
(For guidance on answering this type of question, see pages 48–49.)

# What were the main features of the New Economic Policy?

The New Economic Policy (NEP) was intended by Lenin primarily to meet Russia's urgent need for food. If the peasants could not be forced, then they must be persuaded. He also felt that the new policy would give Russia some breathing space after a period of almost eight years' war. There were some Communists who felt that they were betraying the revolution by reverting back to capitalism.

The NEP also included the electrification of Russia. Lenin was convinced that electrical power was the key to economic growth. A network of power stations started being built in the years after 1921. The NEP also encouraged foreign trade with countries such as Britain. Over the next few years there were large-scale exchanges of Western industrial goods for Russian oil and wheat.

## Key features

The NEP said that:

- Grain requisitioning was abolished. Peasants would still have to give a fixed amount of grain to the government, but they could sell their surplus for profit again.
- Peasants who increased their food production would pay less tax.
- The ban on private trade was removed. This meant that food and goods could flow more easily between the countryside and towns. Privately owned shops were reopened. Rationing was abolished and people had to buy goods and food from their own income. People could use money again and a new rouble was introduced.
- Factories with fewer than twenty workers would be given back to their owners and consumer goods could be produced and sold for profit. This included businesses like small workshops and factories that made goods such as shoes, nails and clothes. Lenin realised that peasants would not sell their produce unless there were goods that they wanted on sale.
- Key industries, such as coal and steel, still remained under state control. The state also retained control of transport and the banking system. Industry was organised into trusts that had to buy materials and pay workers from their own budgets. If they failed to manage their budgets efficiently, they could not expect the state to bail them out.

**Source A** A poster produced by Communist authorities with the aim of promoting the spread of electric power across Russia

## Initial reaction to the NEP

At the Tenth Party Congress in 1921, there was a fierce debate about the NEP. Some party members considered the NEP as a betrayal of the principles of the October Revolution. What finally persuaded the doubters was the Kronstadt Mutiny. They realised that splits in the party could result in them losing power altogether. There was a genuine desire for unity and they were prepared to support Lenin, as long as the NEP was, as Lenin promised, a 'temporary' measure.

**Source B** From a speech by Lenin to party members in March 1921

*We are now retreating, going back as it were, but we are doing this so as to retreat first and then run and leap forward more vigorously. We retreated on this one condition alone when we introduced our New Economic Policy ... so as to begin a more determined offensive after the retreat.*

**Source C** From a speech by Bukharin, a leading Communist and a strong supporter of the NEP, 1922

*Poor, starving old Russia. Russia of primitive lighting and the meal of a crust bread is going to be covered by a network of electric power stations. The NEP will transform the Russian economy and rebuild a broken nation. The future is endless and beautiful.*

**Source D** From *From Lenin to Stalin* written in 1937 by Victor Serge, 1957. Serge became a Bolshevik in 1919 but was expelled from the party in 1928 by Stalin for criticising his policies. Here he is attacking the NEP

*In just a few years, the NEP restored to Russia an aspect of prosperity. But to many of us this prosperity was sometimes distasteful ... we felt ourselves sinking into the mire – paralysed, corrupted ... There was gambling, drunkenness and all the old filth of former times ... Classes were re-born under our eyes ... There was a growing gap between the prosperity of the few and the misery of the many.*

### TASKS

1. How useful is Source A to a historian studying the introduction of electrification in Russia?
   (For guidance on answering this type of question, see pages 59–60.)
2. Describe the key features of the NEP.
   (For guidance on answering this type of question, see page 79.)
3. Use the information from Source B and your own knowledge to explain why Lenin introduced the NEP.
   (For guidance on answering this type of question, see page 40.)
4. Why do Sources C and D have different views about the NEP?
   (For guidance on answering this type of question, see pages 69–70.)

# How successful was the New Economic Policy?

At the end of 1922 the Union of Soviet Socialist Republics (USSR) had been formally established. The NEP had mixed results for the newly created USSR.

## Achievements

By 1922, the results of the NEP were better than anyone had expected.

- There was food in the markets in the cities and a growing trade in other goods.
- Shops, cafés and restaurants reopened.
- By 1923 cereal production had increased by 23 per cent compared to 1920.
- There was a rapid growth in industrial activity, especially from small-scale enterprises. From 1920 to 1923, factory output rose by almost 200 per cent.
- Private traders known as '**Nepmen**' appeared. They bought up produce such as grain, meat, eggs and vegetables to take into the markets of the cities. They travelled round the workshops picking up nails, shoes, clothes and hand tools to sell in the markets. By 1923, Nepmen handled about three-quarters of the retail trade. By 1923, there were 25,000 private traders in Moscow alone.
- Peasants did well out of the NEP. After the famine, there was rapid recovery in the villages. A great deal of trade in produce and handcrafted goods was encouraged between the villages. Peasants were also able to make money on the side in the cities through the Nepmen. They were able to farm their land without much interference from the government.

## Shortcomings of the NEP

Debate about the NEP continued throughout its existence. However, when Lenin died in 1924, the debate was set to become even fiercer within the Communist Party. Trotsky described the NEP as the 'first sign of the degeneration of Bolshevism'. One joke had it that the letters NEP stood for 'New Exploitation of the Proletariat'.

- Those who criticised the NEP said that greed and selfishness were returning to Russia. Nepmen and ***kulaks*** went against the ideals of the October

**Source A** Agricultural and industrial recovery during the NEP

| | 1921 | 1922 | 1923 | 1924 | 1925 |
|---|---|---|---|---|---|
| **Agriculture** | | | | | |
| Sown area (millions of hectares) | 90.3 | 77.7 | 91.7 | 98.1 | 104.3 |
| Grain harvest (millions of tonnes) | 37.6 | 50.3 | 56.6 | 51.4 | 72.5 |
| **Industry** | | | | | |
| Coal (millions of tonnes) | 8.9 | 9.5 | 13.7 | 16.1 | 18.1 |
| Steel (thousands of tonnes) | 183 | 39 | 709 | 1140 | 2135 |
| Finished cloth (millions of metres) | 105 | 349 | 691 | 963 | 1688 |
| Value of factory output (millions of roubles) | 2004 | 2619 | 4005 | 4660 | 7739 |
| Electricity (millions of kWh) | 520 | 775 | 1146 | 1562 | 2925 |
| Rail freight carried (millions of tonnes) | 39.4 | 39.9 | 58.0 | 67.5 | 83.4 |
| Average monthly wage of urban worker (in roubles) | 10.2 | 12.2 | 15.9 | 20.8 | 25.2 |

Revolution and were part of this new get-rich-quick, increasingly capitalist society.

- The NEP encouraged corruption and vice because of the new-found wealth for some people. Prostitution and crime flourished. The Moscow municipal government got most of its income from taxes on gambling clubs, which were a symbol of this new decadence.
- By 1923, so much food was flooding into the cities that the prices started to drop while the prices of industrial goods rose because they were still in short supply. Trotsky called this the 'scissors' crisis'. He likened the economic problem created by the widening gap between industrial and agricultural goods to the open blades of a pair of scissors. It made the peasants reluctant to buy industrial goods. The crisis did not last long as the government took action to bring the price of industrial goods down.

**Source B** Photograph of Nepmen in Smolensk market, 1921

**Source C** Written in the 1980s by Leonid Orlov, a Bolshevik supporter who is remembering life in Russia in the early 1920s

*There wasn't a scrap of food in the country. We were down to a quarter of a pound (114 g) of bread per person. Then suddenly they announced the NEP. Cafés started opening as well as restaurants. Factories went back into private hands. It was capitalism. In my eyes what was happening was the very thing I'd struggled against.*

**Source D** A graph showing the 'scissors' crisis'

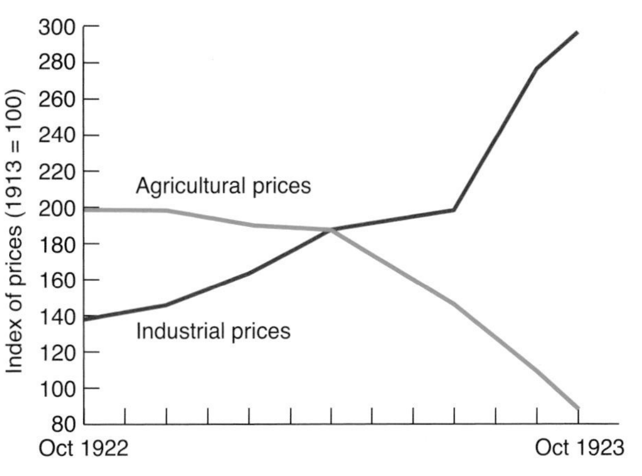


## TASKS

1 What does Source B show you about the effects of the NEP? (For guidance on answering this type of question, see page 22.)

2 Working in pairs, study Sources A to D (pages 88–89) and make a copy of the following grid. Which sources suggest the NEP was a success or a failure? Give a brief explanation for each decision.

| Source | Success | Failure |
|---|---|---|
| A | | |
| B | | |
| C | | |
| D | | |

3 Which of the following statements best sums up the NEP? Give reasons for your choice.

- The NEP was a popular and successful policy.
- The NEP was an unpopular but successful policy.
- The NEP was an unpopular and unsuccessful policy.

4 How successful was the New Economic Policy? (For guidance on answering this type of question, see page 113.)

# Examination guidance

This section provides guidance on how to answer an 'explain' question. This is worth 5 marks.

Explain why Lenin introduced the New Economic Policy. (5 marks)

## Tips on how to answer

- Aim to give a variety of reasons which are well explained.
- The more reasons you can mention the better your chances of scoring the higher marks.
- Most importantly, these reasons need to be supported with relevant factual detail.
- Avoid generalised comments as these will cause you to be awarded low marks.
- Always support your statements with examples.
- Make sure the information you include is directly relevant. Does it answer the question?

### Response by candidate

*The effects of the policy of War Communism caused Lenin to introduce the New Economic Policy. By 1921 the economy was in ruins. Industrial output had fallen sharply and many workers had fled to the countryside. The shortage of food resulted in terrible famine and between 1920 and 1921 over five million Russians died of starvation. There was growing unrest against Bolshevik rule and this caused Lenin to realise that if his party was to stay in power they would have to abandon unpopular policies. Workers in Petrograd went on strike early in 1921 and in February the sailors at the Kronstadt naval base mutinied. They demanded better conditions and the end to War Communism. Lenin responded with the NEP.*

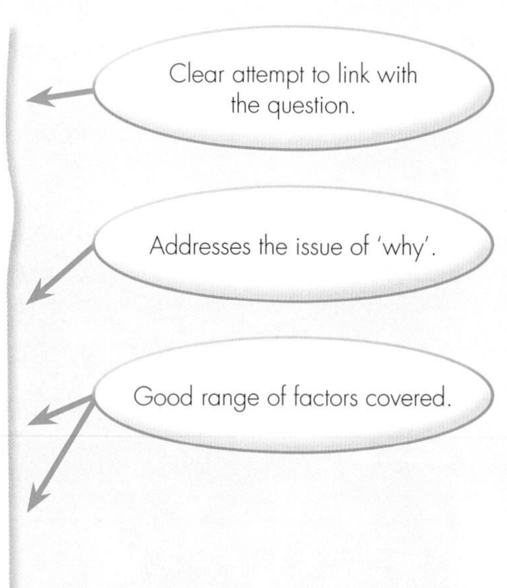


### Examiner's comment

The answer identifies a number of specific reasons and these are explained in some depth. Generalised and descriptive comments have been avoided. There is a clear focus and a good depth of knowledge and understanding is demonstrated. It is worthy of the maximum of 5 marks.

### Now you have a go

Explain why there was growing opposition to Bolshevik rule by 1921. (5 marks)

# 8 Did Lenin succeed in establishing a Communist state in Russia?

**Source A**
A photograph of the Agitprop or cinema carriage of a Red Army propaganda train in 1923

In the years 1921–24, Lenin established a Communist dictatorship in Russia, partly through the use of the *Cheka* and terror but also through propaganda and increasingly centralised control of all aspects of everyday life including culture, education and the economy. This Communist control, in turn, brought rapid changes in the position of women and religion in Russia. Furthermore, there were changes in the organisation and influence of the Communist Party in the Soviet Union, especially with the setting up of the **Comintern**.

This chapter answers the following questions:

- How did Lenin create the organs of the Communist state?
- How did centralisation increase under Lenin's leadership?
- What was life like under Communist rule?

## TASK

What does Source A tell you about propaganda methods used by the Communists?

(For guidance on answering this type of question, see page 22.)

### Examination guidance

Throughout this chapter you will be given the opportunity to practise different exam-style questions and detailed guidance on how to answer an essay question which provides a scaffold to help you structure your answer. This is worth 10 marks.

# How did Lenin create the organs of the Communist state?

Lenin was able to create a dictatorship of the Communist Party in the years after the October Revolution.

## The organisation of the Communist Party in the Soviet Union (CPSU)

The Union of Soviet Socialist Republics (USSR) or the Soviet Union was officially set up in 1922. This included areas occupied by the Red Army during the Civil War as well as areas with a history of independence such as Georgia and the Ukraine.

The Communist Party controlled the government at every level. Key officials in the government were members of the Communist Party. Senior members of the government were usually senior members of the party. The diagram opposite shows how the party, otherwise known as the CPSU (Communist Party in the Soviet Union), was organised.

## The government of the USSR

The government was controlled by the Communist Party at all levels:

- Key officials in the government were members of the Communist Party.
- Senior members of the government were usually senior members of the party.

The diagram on page 93 shows how the government of the USSR was organised.

## The Comintern

In January 1919, Lenin called for an international congress of revolutionary socialists. Two months later, 35 groups met in Moscow and the Communist International or Comintern was set up. The Comintern appealed to the workers of all countries to support the Soviet regime by all available means, including, if necessary, 'revolutionary means'.

The second Comintern congress took place in 1920 and included representatives from 41 countries. Lenin attempted to bring foreign Communist parties under Comintern (Bolshevik) control by imposing 21 conditions for membership including the stipulation that Communist parties had to be organised on Leninist principles of central control and discipline. However, the Comintern had limited success.

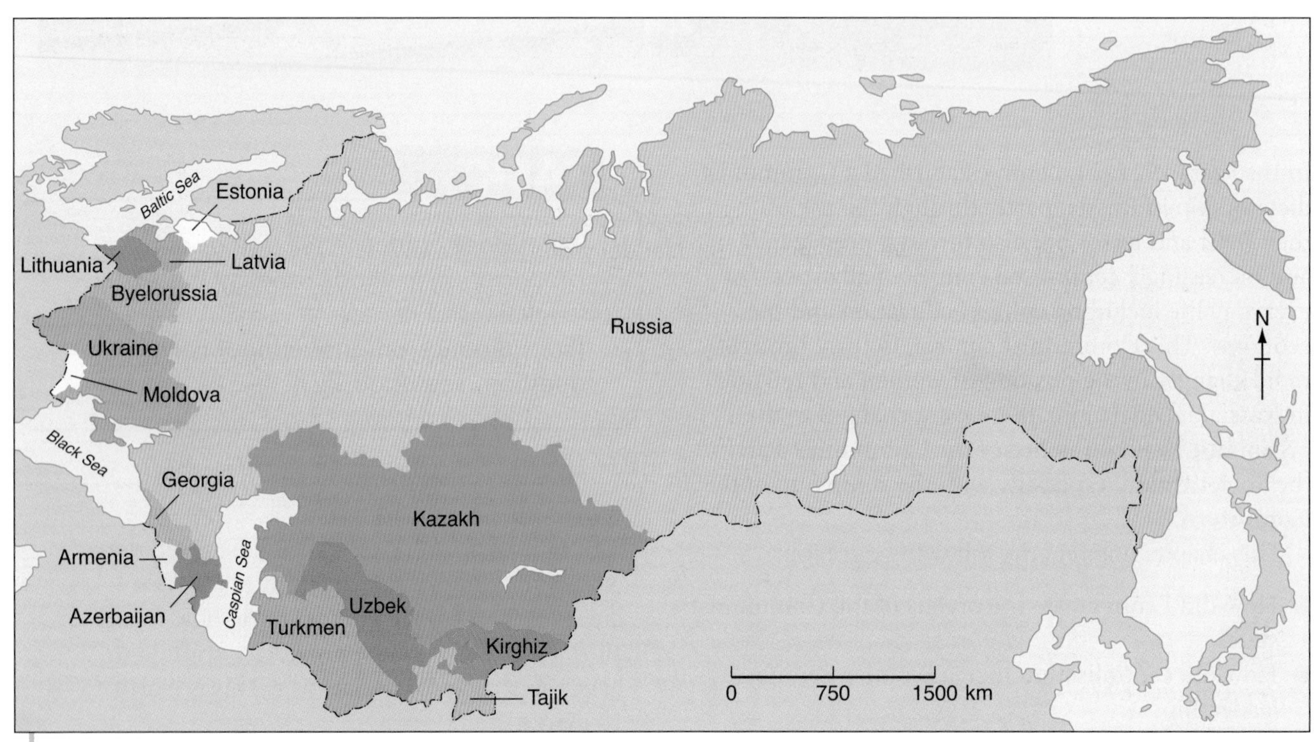


A map showing the USSR in 1922

- Communist uprisings in Germany and Hungary were failures.
- Communist parties in other countries resented control from Moscow.
- It did much to worsen relations with other countries, especially Britain. For example, the British Foreign Secretary, Curzon, was so infuriated by the activities of Comintern agents in Persia, Afghanistan and India, that he threatened to cancel the Anglo-Soviet trade agreement in 1921 unless they abandoned these activities. The Soviets agreed to accept the 'Curzon ultimatum'.

## How the CPSU was organised

***Politburo***
This was the leading decision-making body of the Communist Party. It was set up in 1919 and made all the key decisions. It met on a daily basis and included between seven and nine members chosen by the Central Committee

**The Central Committee**
This had 30–40 members and ran party affairs when congresses were not sitting. It was the main party body until 1919 and continued to discuss key issues in the 1920s. However, major decisions were increasingly made by the *Politburo*

**Congress**
This consisted of representatives from city and regional party organisations. It debated issues and voted on the main policies. In 1921, Lenin introduced a 'ban on factions' which meant that once party policy was agreed by the Central Committee then all party members had to accept it. In reality, this meant that few decisions were now questioned

**City and provincial parties**
Party secretaries at this level often had powerful positions. Kamenev, for example, got much of his support from his control of Moscow. The central party organisation took a keen interest in appointing party members at this level, especially after Stalin became general secretary in 1921 (see page 106). Delegates to congress came from this level

**Local parties**
Many people joined local parties because of the benefits they could get from being a party member. For example, this could lead to election to the local or district soviet or other local government jobs

## How the government of the USSR was organised

**The Council of People's Commissars (*Sovnarkom*)**
Around 15–20 members under Lenin, who was chairman. Members came from the Central Executive Committee. This met daily and was the key decision-making body

**Central Executive Committee**
This was elected by the Congress of Soviets. It organised the administration of the government but had little power

**All-Russian Congress of Soviets**
Delegates were elected by city and provincial soviets. It met twice a year and was the supreme law-making authority

**Provincial and city soviets**
Members were elected from local and district soviets. They were responsible for the administration of larger cities and fed back to the Central Executive Committee the needs and problems of the regions and cities

**Local and district soviets**
This was the lowest level of soviets. It included representatives from local areas such as smaller cities and towns. They were the point of contact for people who wanted to put their views and needs to a higher level

**TASKS**

**1** Describe how the Communist Party (CPSU) was organised.
(For guidance on answering this type of question, see page 79.)

**2** Describe how the government of the USSR was organised.
(For guidance on answering this type of question, see page 79.)

**3** Explain why Lenin set up the Comintern.
(For guidance on answering this type of question, see page 90.)

## The *Cheka* and the Red Terror

The systematic use of terror was used by Lenin to back up any new measures, remove any opposition to the Bolshevik regime and establish a one-party state (see page 95).

**Source A** From a letter written by Lenin to a Bolshevik leader in Penza in 1919

*Hang no fewer than a hundred well-known kulaks, richbags and blood-suckers and make sure the hanging takes place in full view of the people.*

The Red Terror was launched by the *Cheka* in the summer of 1918 to terrify all hostile social groups. Its victims included large numbers of workers and peasants as well as princes, priests, judges, merchants, traders and even children.

- In the cities, *Cheka* arrests were often of a terrifyingly random nature; for example, for being near scenes of '**bourgeois** provocation' or simply being an acquaintance of a suspect.
- The *Cheka* was even more active in the countryside, supporting requisition brigades to collect grain from the peasants.
- The *Cheka* imprisoned opponents in concentration and labour camps.

**Source B** From an interview given by Dzerzhinsky, the leader of the *Cheka*, to the press in 1918

*The Cheka is the defence of the revolution as the Red Army is; as in the civil war, the Red Army cannot stop to ask whether it may harm particular individuals, but must take into account only one thing, the victory of the revolution over the bourgeoisie. So the Cheka must defend the revolution and conquer the enemy even if its sword falls occasionally on the innocent.*

**Source C** From *Memoirs of a British Agent* by Bruce Lockhart published in 1932. Lockhart was in Moscow in 1918 and describes what he saw when being questioned by the *Cheka* in August 1918

*As we were talking a motor van pulled up in the courtyard below. There was a scream. Then the fat figure of a priest was half pushed and half carried to the van. His terror was pitiful. Tears rolled down his face. His knees rocked and he fell, like a great ball of fat, on the ground. I felt sick and turned away. It was the notorious Bishop Vostorgoff, one of the several hundred victims of the terror who were shot at the time as revenge for the attempted assassination of Lenin.*

**TASKS**

**4** What does Source A tell you about the *Cheka* and the Red Terror?

**5** Why do Sources B and C have different views about the *Cheka* and the Red Terror?
(For guidance on answering this type of question, see pages 69–70.)

# How did centralisation increase under Lenin's leadership?

By 1924, the USSR was governed by a centralised, one-party dictatorship which did not permit anyone to challenge its power. A large part of the economy – industry, banking, transport and foreign trade – was controlled by the government. This was partly due to Lenin's attempts to create a Communist state but mainly as a result of the necessities of the Civil War.

## TASKS

1 Describe how the Communist government centralised its control of the economy.
(For guidance on answering this type of question, see page 79.)

2 Explain why the Bolsheviks introduced central control of the economy.
(For guidance on answering this type of question, see page 90.)

### Industry

By the summer of 1918, industrial output had fallen dramatically. It was essential to keep industries going during the Civil War, so the government nationalised industry. Industry was under the control of ***Vesenkha*** or the Supreme Economic Council which reported directly to *Sovnarkom* – the Council of People's Commissars. By the autumn of 1919, it was estimated that 80 per cent of enterprises were controlled by the government. The NEP did return factories with fewer than twenty workers to their owners, but left the major industries under state control (see page 86).

### Banking

The Decree on Banking, December 1917, nationalised all the banks which were now controlled by *Sovnarkom*.

**Bolshevik centralisation**

### Transport

The Bolsheviks also took control of transport, more especially the railway system. This was essential for the war effort and to maintain food supplies to cities.

### Foreign trade

The Bolsheviks also centrally controlled all foreign trade. However, there was little or no trade during the Civil War due to opposition in the West to communism. However, the introduction of the NEP encouraged Lenin to develop trade links with the West. In 1921, the Anglo-Russian trade treaty reopened trade links between the two. Both sides agreed not to engage in hostile propaganda. Additionally, the Soviets recognised (in principle), their obligation to pay firms in Britain for goods supplied to Russia during the war.

# What was life like under Communist rule?

There was considerable change for many under Communist rule in the years 1918–24.

## Changes for women

There were a number of changes for women, some of which actually worsened their position while others improved their position.

### *Marriage*

Lenin was convinced that the traditional married role of women was nothing better than slavery, with wives the property of their husbands. He passed a series of laws:

- New divorce law which made it far easier to get a divorce.
- Guaranteed paid maternity leave two months before and after the birth.
- In 1920 abortion on demand was made legal in all state hospitals. The USSR became the first country to legalise abortion. Before that, many women had died or been seriously injured in back-street operations.
- Church weddings were replaced with civil marriages which reduced the influence of religion.

Lenin felt that the Soviet government had done more than any other country to emancipate women. However:

- In 1919, the USSR had the highest marriage rate yet, by the mid-1920s, the highest divorce rate in Europe, 25 times higher than Britain. By 1927, two-thirds of marriages in Moscow ended in divorce.
- With easy divorce available, many women were abandoned when they became pregnant. Seventy per cent of divorces were initiated by men.

### *Employment*

In employment, if anything, the position of women worsened. During the First World War, the number of women working in industry doubled. However, after the Civil War, with five million men discharged from military service, women suffered as men were given preference for jobs. Indeed, with the growth of urban unemployment during the NEP, women were forced from skilled to unskilled work, mainly in textiles and domestic service, or unemployment. Furthermore, women in employment often worked an eight-hour day outside the home plus an extra five hours in domestic tasks, as traditionally men did not help in the home.

### *Politics*

The Communist Party stressed the equality of women in politics. In 1919 the Party set up a Woman's Department of the *Sovnarkom* called the ***Zhenotdel***. Its leader, Alexandra Kollontai, was the first woman ever to be a member of a European government. In practice, *Zhenotdel* focused on practical help such as social services and education rather than increased political participation. In reality, women made little progress in politics because of male chauvinism. There were even reports of women being attacked or beaten up by their husbands for being involved in party work.

- In 1917, women formed ten per cent of party membership. By 1928 this had increased only slightly to twelve per cent.
- At the party congress of 1918, only five per cent of the voting delegates were women. The numbers actually fell over the next six years.

**Source A** From an interview with a Communist Party official in 1930

*In principle we separated marriage from economics, in principle we destroyed the family hearth, but we carried out the resolution on marriage in such a manner that only the man benefited from it. The woman remains tied with chains to the destroyed family hearth. The man, happily whistling, can leave it, abandoning the women and children.*

**Source B** A woman delegate speaking at a party congress in 1923. She complained that her husband forbade her to take part in politics

*And in those very meetings which he forbids me to attend because he is afraid I will become a real person – what he needs is a cook and mistress wife – in those very meetings where I have to slip in secretly, he makes thunderous speeches about the role of women in the revolution, calls women to a more active role.*

## TASKS

**1** What message does Source A give about the effects of Communist rule on women?

**2** Describe the changes in marriage under the Bolsheviks. (For guidance on answering this type of question, see page 79.)

**3** Use the information in Source B and your own knowledge to explain why women made little progress under Communist rule. (For guidance on answering this type of question, see page 40.)

**4** Working in pairs, make a copy of the following table and complete to show changes in the position of women under the Communists.

| | Better | Worse |
|---|---|---|
| Marriage | | |
| Employment | | |
| Politics | | |

Overall, did the position of women improve under the Bolsheviks?

## Control over education

In the 1919 Communist Party programme, education was defined as 'an instrument for the Communist transformation of society'. This was achieved through control of education. Each child was to receive nine years of free, universal education schooling and youth organisations and the setting up of state-controlled youth organisations.

### *Schooling*

Schools were placed under the Commissariat for Enlightenment.

- The curriculum was changed to include compulsory learning about the history of revolution and communism.
- There was more practical education, focusing on technical subjects and industrial training, with visits to factories, state farms and power stations.
- The authority of teachers was reduced and they were designated as 'school workers'. They were forbidden to set homework or discipline pupils. This led to a lack of authority and discipline in the schools.
- The financial pressure under the NEP meant that the idea of universal schooling had to be abandoned. Many children left school and, by 1923, the number of schools and pupils was barely half that of two years earlier.

### *Youth organisations*

Two youth organisations were set up to capture the hearts and minds of the young through the indoctrination of Communist ideas.

- The Pioneers was for children under fifteen and was very much like the Boy Scouts with activities, trips and camping.
- The ***Komsomol*** was for young people from the age of fifteen until the early twenties. This was much more serious and was used by the Communists to take propaganda into the towns and villages through *Komsomol* activities. *Komsomol* membership was seen as a preparation for entry into the Communist Party.

**Source C** A photograph of members of the Pioneers in 1922

## TASKS

**5** What does Source C show you about the Communist youth movement? (For guidance on answering this type of question, see page 22.)

**6** Describe the changes in education under the Communists. (For guidance on answering this type of question, see page 79.)

## Culture

The Bolsheviks wanted to control all aspects of culture but had limited success in the years 1917–24. Following the October Revolution, they set up the Commissariat of Public Enlightenment headed by Anatoly Lunacharsky. He was determined to move away from the 'high art' of the privileged classes – ballet, opera, fine art – to cultural activities which would appeal to a mass audience. He wanted a collective culture which encouraged workers to produce their own culture.

This new collective culture was known as ***Proletkult*** (proletariat cultural movement) and was the idea of Lunacharsky's brother-in-law, Alexander Bogdanov. Some of the more extreme members of *Proletkult* wanted to do away with libraries and art galleries, which were seen as symbols of the bourgeois culture of the past. Bogdanov set up studios, poetry circles, folk theatres and exhibitions to encourage the masses to participate in other aspects of culture.

### *Art*

Lunacharsky wanted to use art as a form of propaganda and was eager to keep well-known artists on the side of communism. A new style of art, known as **avant-garde**, emerged at the end of the First World War. Avant-garde artists saw themselves as revolutionaries overturning existing ideas about art – stripping it to its bare essentials. Many of these artists joined the Bolsheviks, and produced posters supporting them.

However, Lenin had no use for avant-garde art because it was neither loved nor understood by the people. He much preferred a group of artists who were known as the Association of Artists of Revolutionary Russia who promised 'We will depict the life of the Red Army, the workers, the peasants and the heroes of labour'. This heroic realism, which was later known as '**Socialist Realism**', was exactly what Lenin had in mind. This art was far more optimistic and showed happy workers, working for the victory of communism. The bad side of life was never shown. It was the duty of art to make sure that the message of the revolution was understood by everyone.

**Source D** Lenin's views on art, 1919

*Art belongs to the people. It should be understood and loved by these people. It should bring together the thought and will of these people and elevate them.*

### *Writers*

Lenin's government wanted to control writers in Russia and ensure that what was written praised communism. This policy was not very effective in the 1920s. Writers were allowed to write more or less what they wanted, unless it was regarded as counter-revolutionary. Well-known writers continued for a number of years to write as they had done before the revolution.

## Religion

The Bolsheviks were **atheists** and saw religion as a sign of backwardness. Lenin even said that 'Electricity will take the place of God. Let the peasants pray to electricity. They are going to feel the power of the central authorities more than that of heaven'. However, because the vast majority of Russians were deeply religious, Lenin allowed freedom of worship and belief, while aiming to destroy the power and wealth of the Church.

**Source E** A photograph of a church being looted by Red Army soldiers, 1918

The following flowchart shows the Bolshevik policies towards religion.

*Decree on the Separation of the Church and State*
Issued in January 1918 by the Bolsheviks. This declared that the Church could not own property and banned all religious education in schools

*The Union of the Militant Godless*
This was set up in 1921 with branches all over the country. It held debates to prove that God did not exist and had its own newspaper which attacked the priests as fat parasites living off the peasants

*Direct action*
Lenin used the famine of 1921–22 to demand that the Church surrender its valuables. Instructions were sent to local soviets to seize these valuables. However, there was very strong resistance. Unarmed civilians, often older men and women, fought soldiers equipped with machine guns. More than 8000 people were executed during this anti-Church campaign

## Propaganda and censorship

Immediately after the October Revolution, Lenin set up the Commissariat of Popular Enlightenment and used censorship and propaganda to try to ensure that the majority of Russians supported Communist ideas. Censorship was imposed immediately after the October Revolution but was more rigorously imposed in the years 1917–24.

- In November 1917, the Decree on the Press banned all non-Bolshevik newspapers.
- In the spring of 1922, dozens of outstanding Russian writers and scholars were deported to show people that it was not a good idea to criticise the government.
- In 1922 pre-publication censorship was introduced. Books, articles, poems and writings had to be submitted to the Main Administration for the Affairs of Literature and Publishing Houses before they could be published.

**Source F** A photograph of an Agitprop train in 1919

## TASKS

**7** How important was propaganda and censorship to the Bolsheviks after 1921?
(For guidance on answering this type of question, see page 113.)

**8** Use the information in Source D and your own knowledge, to explain why Lenin supported the realist style of art.
(For guidance on answering this type of question, see page 40.)

**9** What does Source E show you about the treatment of religion under the Communists?
(For guidance on answering this type of question, see page 22.)

**10** Describe how the Bolsheviks reduced the wealth and power of the Russian Church.
(For guidance on answering this type of question, see page 79.)

## Methods of propaganda

Various methods were used to put across Bolshevik ideas.

**Posters**
The street poster was used to get the Bolshevik message across to every corner of the Russian Empire. The message had to be simple and visual because many Russians could not read or write. ***Pravda***, the Bolshevik newspaper, claimed that they produced 375,000 posters in 1919 alone. Many posters included the notice:

ANYONE WHO TEARS DOWN OR COVERS THIS POSTER IS COMMITTING A COUNTER-REVOLUTIONARY ACT

**Cinema**
The Bolsheviks made use of the cinema to put across their ideas to the masses. However, cinemas were almost entirely restricted to the towns so the government introduced specially equipped trains which travelled around Russia showing political propaganda films (see Source F, page 99). The Department for Agitation and Propaganda, shortened to Agitprop, was set up to organise stage plays, pamphlets, motion pictures and other art forms with an explicitly political message. Agitprop trains and boats toured the country, with artists and actors performing simple plays and broadcasting propaganda. They had a printing press on board the train to allow posters to be reproduced and thrown out of the windows when it passed through villages. In the early 1920s, a special unit, *Proletkino*, was set up to make political films. Eisenstein was the best-known Soviet film director of the twentieth century. His first film was *Strike* (1924), with a clear message about how workers were oppressed and how they could resist

**Propaganda**

**Street processions and theatre**
The Bolsheviks made use of the rich tradition of street festivals. May Day and the anniversary of the October Revolution became the great annual festivals. Street theatre was used, with the most famous example being in October 1920 with the re-enactment of the storming the Winter Palace involving 10,000 people and the Winter Palace itself

**Statues and banners**
Massive banners were placed in towns and cities. Moscow City Soviet was draped with the huge banner 'The proletariat has nothing to lose but its chains'. Lenin also wanted huge statues of revolutionaries and provided a list of 66 names, including Marx and Engels

## TASKS

**11** What does Source F (see page 99) show you about the agitprop trains? (For guidance on answering this type of question, see page 22.)

**12** How effective do you think each method of propaganda or censorship would have been? Make a copy of the following table and give your verdict on each method, with a brief explanation. One example has been done for you.

| | Very effective | Effective | Quite effective | Not effective |
|---|---|---|---|---|
| **Posters** | Easily seen and understood | | | |
| **Cinema** | | | | |
| **Processions** | | | | |
| **Street theatre** | | | | |
| **Statues and banners** | | | | |

# Examination guidance

This section provides guidance on how to answer an essay question which provides a scaffold to help you structure your answer. The question carries 10 marks and up to an additional 3 marks will be awarded for spelling, punctuation and grammar (SPaG).

Had Lenin succeeded in establishing a strong Communist state by 1924? (10 marks)

In your answer you should:

- discuss the measures which helped Lenin to create a strong Communist state
- discuss any measures which suggest the Communist state was not so strong.

There is a candidate response to this question and examiner's comment about it on page 102.

## Tips on how to answer

- You need to develop an answer which has balance and good support.
- You should start by discussing the factor mentioned in the question, using your factual knowledge to explain why this factor is important.
- You then need to consider the counter-argument by using your knowledge to examine other relevant factors.
- These points need to be discussed in some detail, starting a new paragraph for each point.
- Aim to link the paragraphs by using words such as 'other factors include', 'also important', 'in addition to', 'however'.
- Avoid generalised comments – the more specific your observations the higher mark you will get, providing the factual information is relevant to the question.
- Conclude your answer with a link back to the question, making a judgement about the importance of the factor listed in the question when ranked against the other factors you have discussed.
- You should aim to write between one and two sides of a sheet.
- You need to remember that you will be awarded marks for good spelling, punctuation and grammar (SPaG). Remember to use capital letters, paragraphs and full sentences.

## Response by candidate

*By the time of his death in 1924 Lenin had succeeded in establishing the key features of a strong Communist state. Under his leadership the Bolsheviks had defeated the Whites in the Civil War and dismissed all opposition within the nation. The Bolsheviks created a strong one-party state in Russia headed by the Communist Party. The CPSU controlled government at every level and all government officials had to be a member of the Communist Party. Lenin headed the Politburo which was a small decision-making body which directed the main affairs of the state, taking over from the Sovnakom by the early 1920s. The Cheka was used to eliminate any political opposition and the Bolsheviks made great use of censorship and propaganda to spread their ideology. Lenin introduced policies which resulted in a growth of centralisation with increasing state control over the banks and finance, and for a time industry and agriculture. Communist ideology was introduced into everyday life. The Marriage Law gave women more freedom, allowing them to marry and divorce more easily and granting them the right to have abortions on demand. Women also gained equality in the workplace. Education was heavily under Communist control and there was a huge campaign to improve literacy. A Young Communist League (the Komsomol) was established to encourage the growth of Communist ideas among the young.*

*However, there were some areas where Lenin was less successful in enforcing Communist ideology. Opposition to the policy of War Communism meant that he had to introduce the NEP which many saw as a betrayal of true Communist ideas. It introduced the idea of free enterprise and resulted in the emergence of Nepmen and kulaks, creating a state which had non-Communist class divisions. Lenin also failed to ban religion outright and was forced to adopt a middle way. He failed to change the religious beliefs of Russians and over 90 per cent remained Orthodox Christians by 1924. When he died in 1924, Lenin had failed to appoint a successor and this caused a power struggle between several rivals, most notably Stalin and Trotsky, which undermined the strength of the Communist state.*

*Overall, Lenin had succeeded in laying the foundations of a strong Communist state which Stalin developed further. However, in order for the Communist Party to survive in the early 1920s he had been forced to introduce some non-Communist policies such as the NEP which weakened the enforcement of Communist ideology.*

Introduction which links to the question.

Deals with the key factor mentioned in the question, providing precise details.

Begins the counter-argument. Using the term 'however' makes it clear you are now looking at other factors.

Other factors are discussed such as the NEP and religion, but the range is narrow.

Attempts a reasoned conclusion which provides a judgement on the question set.

### Examiner's comment

The candidate has produced a reasoned and supported answer which matches the criteria for a level 4 response. Support for the key issue is strong, and a range of factors have been included to illustrate the creation of a powerful Communist state. A counter-argument is offered but the range of examples to support it is narrow. For this reason it was awarded low level 4 (9 marks) as the answer lacked an overall balance. The response was well written with good use of specialist terms and accurate spelling, punctuation and grammar (SPaG). The full mark weighting of 3 was awarded for SPaG.

# What was Lenin's legacy to Russia?

Lenin died in 1924 following a series of strokes. There followed a struggle to decide who would succeed him as leader. Trotsky was by far the favourite due to his leadership of the Red Army and his achievements in the years 1917–24. Stalin was very much the outsider. He was not well known outside party circles, nor did he have Trotsky's intellect and experience. Nevertheless, through a combination of his own shrewdness and Trotsky's overconfidence and weaknesses, Stalin became eventual leader.

This chapter will answer the following questions:

- Why was there a power struggle to succeed Lenin?
- Who were the leadership rivals?
- How did the rivals struggle for power?
- Why was Stalin favourite to succeed Lenin by the end of 1924?
- What was Lenin's legacy to Russia?

**Source A** An account of Lenin's death which appeared in the *Manchester Guardian*, a British newspaper, on 22 January 1924

*Lenin had a sudden relapse yesterday, became unconscious, and died an hour later, just before seven in the evening. When Congress met at eleven this morning, Kalinin, who was hardly able to speak, announced Lenin's death in a few broken sentences. Almost everybody in the great theatre burst into tears, and from all parts came the hysterical wailing of women. Tears were running down the faces of the members of the Congress. The funeral march of the Revolutionaries was played by a weeping orchestra. It was announced that January 21 will be a day of mourning in the Russian calendar.*

Examination guidance

Throughout this chapter you will be given the opportunity to practise different exam-style questions.

**TASK**

What can you learn about Lenin's death from Source A?

# Why was there a power struggle to succeed Lenin?

On 30 August 1918, there was an attempt to assassinate Lenin. He was shot twice by Dora Kaplan, a Socialist Revolutionary, who said that she had done so because she considered Lenin a 'traitor to the revolution'. Lenin was severely wounded and one of the bullets entered his neck. Doctors were unable to remove it because it was too close to his spine. However, Lenin made a quick recovery and the Bolshevik press declared it a miracle. He continued to work extremely hard; his working day was 16 hours – seven days a week. In 1921, he began to complain of headaches and exhaustion.

**Source A** From the Bolshevik newspaper *Krasnaya Gazeta*, just after the assassination attempt on Lenin, 1 September 1918

*Without mercy, we will kill our enemies in scores of hundreds. Let them be thousands, let them drown themselves in their own blood. For the blood of Lenin let there be floods of bourgeois blood – more blood, as much as possible.*

On 25 May 1922, Lenin had a stroke which left him partially paralysed on his right side and temporarily unable to speak. His illness meant that he could not take an active role in government for some months. Instead, during the summer of 1922, Russia was ruled by a group of three: Stalin, Zinoviev and Kamenev. Each had designs on the leadership of the country and the three were united by a dislike of Trotsky. In Zinoviev's case, it was an intense hatred.

Lenin resumed limited duties in August and was able to address party meetings. However, he suffered a second stroke on 15 December 1922 and Stalin took control of his welfare. Stalin ensured that no one was permitted to visit him and he was only allowed to dictate notes for a few minutes each day. A third stroke followed on 9 March 1923 and this resulted in almost complete loss of speech – he could only say words of one syllable – and was confined to a wheelchair. Lenin's contribution to Russian politics was over. He died in January 1924.

**Source B** Photograph of Lenin with his sister and one of his doctors, summer 1923

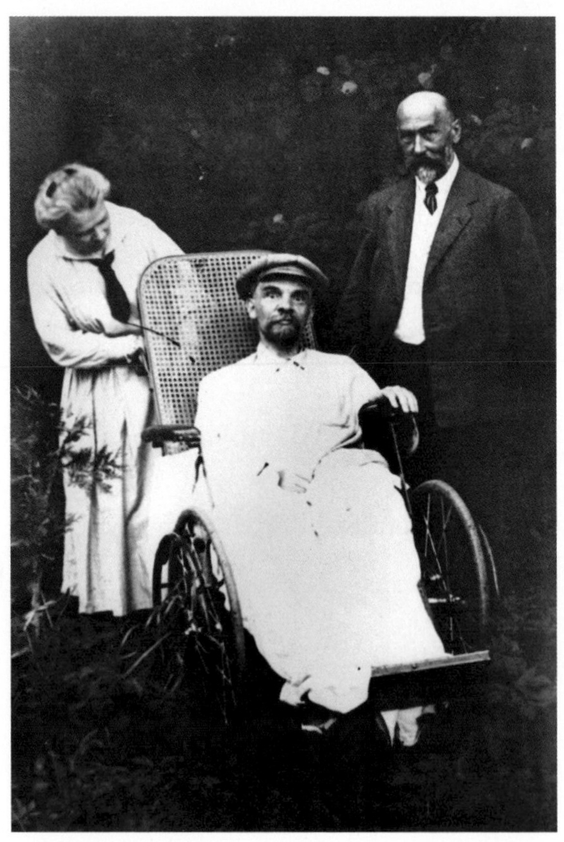

During Lenin's illness, Stalin, Zinoviev and Kamenev agreed to oppose Trotsky in the *Politburo* because they saw him as the most likely to succeed Lenin. Lenin was aware of the tension and was concerned that either a split might develop in the Communist Party or too much power might be concentrated in the hands of one person. Lenin began to put his thoughts together about a possible successor in what eventually became known as his political testament. The testament seemed to show that Lenin wanted a collective leadership. His views were as follows:

**Lenin's testament**

- Trotsky: the ablest but Lenin felt he was drawn to administrative affairs. Lenin also thought he never worked out his ideas to their conclusion.
- Bukharin: was felt not to be sufficiently Marxist.
- Kamenev: criticised for his unwillingness to commit to revolution in 1917.
- Zinoviev: criticised for his unwillingness to commit to revolution in 1917.
- Stalin: felt he had concentrated too much power in his hands as General Secretary.

## TASKS

1. What does Source A tell you about reactions to the attempt on Lenin's life in 1918?
2. How useful is Source B to a historian studying the decline in health of Lenin? (For guidance on answering this type of question, see pages 59–60.)
3. Describe Lenin's decline in health between 1921 and 1924. (For guidance on answering this type of question, see page 79.)
4. Explain why Lenin's political testament was important. (For guidance on answering this type of question, see page 90.)
5. Suggest reasons why the Bolsheviks embalmed Lenin's body (see Source C).

**Source C** Photograph of the embalmed body of Lenin

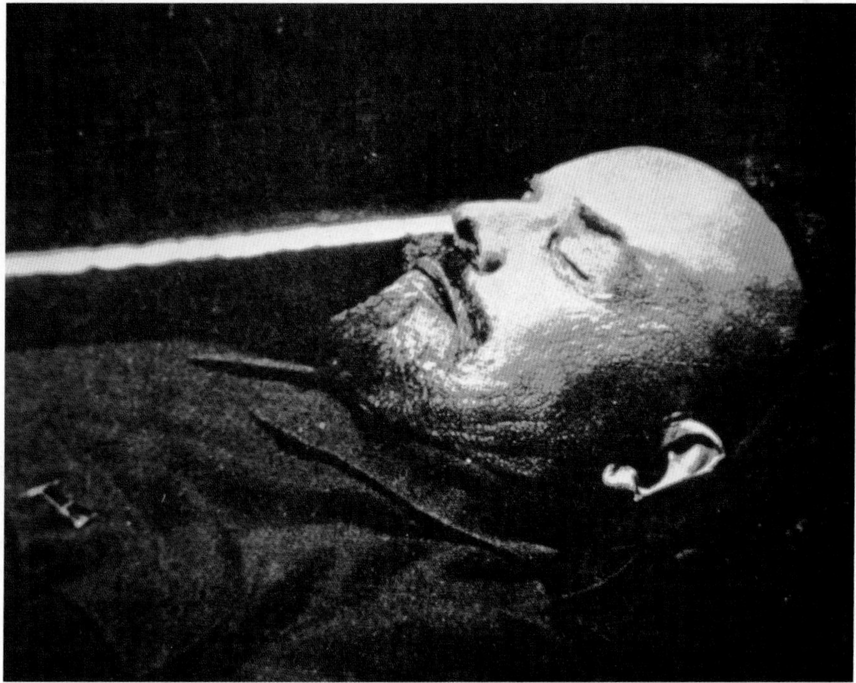

# Who were the leadership rivals?

After Lenin's death several Bolsheviks emerged as contenders to the leadership (see below). However, at the time of his death no decision about his successor had been made. The struggle for the leadership lasted four years and was eventually won by Joseph Stalin.

**Leon Trotsky** (see page 34 for additional biographical details)
- Had helped to organise the Bolshevik Revolution of October 1917
- Led the Red Army to victory in the Civil War
- Commissar for War, leader of the Red Army
- One of the key intellectuals of the Bolshevik Party
- Opposed the NEP
- Argued for permanent revolution

**Grigory Zinoviev**
- Had helped to set up the Bolshevik Party in 1903
- In exile with Lenin until 1917
- Opposed Lenin's proposals for revolution in October 1917
- Bolshevik Party leader in Petrograd after the Revolution
- Head of Comintern, the organisation through which the Bolsheviks hoped to bring about Communist revolutions in other countries
- Opposed the NEP
- Disliked Trotsky

**Lev Kamenev**

- Trotsky's brother-in-law
- Opposed Lenin's proposals for revolution in October 1917
- Leader of the Bolshevik Party in Moscow
- Opposed the NEP
- Disliked Trotsky

**Nikolai Bukharin**

- Acknowledged as the best thinker in the Bolshevik Party
- Had opposed the Treaty of Brest-Litovsk
- Supporter of the New Economic Policy – he was happy for peasants to make a profit
- Editor of the Bolshevik newspaper *Pravda*
- Opposed Trotsky's views after 1924

**Joseph Stalin**
- As a Bolshevik, arrested and exiled to Siberia eight times before the Revolution
- Editor of *Pravda*, the Bolshevik newspaper in 1917
- Commissar of Nationalities in Lenin's government
- Member of the *Politburo* and **Secretariat.** This meant that he helped to make policies, carry them out and above all could oversee members of the party
- In 1922, he was given what was regarded as the most boring and dull of jobs, General Secretary of the Communist Party, responsible for the day-to-day running of the party and the appointment and dismissal of key members
- Organised Lenin's funeral

## TASKS

**1** Work in pairs. One of you is Stalin and the other Trotsky. You are to be interviewed by the *Politburo* members for the job of party leader. Prepare a presentation/speech for your candidate. Remember to stress your strengths and the weaknesses of your opponent.

**2** Lenin has just died and you are a friend and adviser to Trotsky. Write a letter to Trotsky giving him advice on how he can win the leadership.

# How did the rivals struggle for power?

By early 1923, it was clear that the two main contenders for the leadership were Stalin and Trotsky. Lenin's political testament showed he favoured Trotsky (see Source A). However, Stalin was gaining more power throughout 1922 by removing his opponents from the party and replacing them with his own supporters. As Stalin gained more power, Trotsky moved out of the limelight, mainly because he was ill for some of the time. In January 1923, Stalin cleverly suggested that Trotsky be offered the position of Lenin's deputy in *Sovnarkom* (see page 42). Trotsky refused because he was still ill and said that such a position would not help the country or the party. This refusal was seen by Stalin and many Communists as an insult.

**Source A** Lenin's views on the leadership in his political testament, 1923

*Comrade Stalin, having become secretary, has unlimited authority concentrated in his hands and I am not sure whether he will be capable of using that authority with sufficient caution. Comrade Trotsky, on the other hand, is perhaps the most capable man in the present committee. Stalin is too rude and this fault is not acceptable in the office of secretary. Therefore I propose to comrades that they find a way of removing Stalin from his post.*

**Source B** From *A People's Tragedy: The Russian Revolution 1881–1924* by O. Figes, published in 1996

*All the Bolshevik leaders made the same mistake of underestimating Stalin's potential power, and his ambition to exercise it. Lenin was as guilty as the rest. For a man of such intolerance, he proved remarkably tolerant of Stalin's many sins, not least his growing rudeness to himself, in the belief that he needed Stalin to maintain the unity of the party. It was for this reason that he agreed to make Stalin the party's first general secretary.*

**Source C** From Lenin's letter to Stalin, 5 March 1923

*Dear Comrade Stalin: You have been so rude as to summon my wife to the telephone and use bad language ... I have no intention of forgetting so easily what has been done against me, and it goes without saying that what has been done against my wife I consider having been done against me ... make your apologies, or ... relations between us should be broken off.*

## Lenin and Stalin

At the end of 1922, Stalin and Lenin disagreed about issues of international trade. In addition, Lenin was against the way Stalin dealt with the various nationalities in Russia and disliked the way he treated people in meetings. Lenin was horrified when he learnt that one of Stalin's men had beaten up a prominent Georgian Bolshevik leader.

Stalin's relations with Lenin worsened in January 1923, when Stalin and Lenin's wife, Krupskaya, had a disagreement. Lenin demanded an apology from Stalin and threatened to break off personal relations unless one was offered. However, Lenin's second stroke prevented this from going further and Stalin was saved the embarrassment of an apology and disgrace at the forthcoming party congress which was to be held in May.

### TASKS

1. What does Source A tell you about Lenin's view on the succession?
2. Use the information in Source B and your own knowledge to explain why Stalin was in a powerful position to succeed Lenin.
   (For guidance on answering this type of question, see page 40.)
3. Use the information in Source C and your own knowledge to explain the effects of Stalin's behaviour on his relationship with Lenin.
   (For guidance on answering this type of question, see page 40.)

## Lenin's political testament

Following his death, Lenin's political testament was sent to the Bolshevik Central Committee. It was read out in a closed meeting at the party congress in May 1924. The testament meant that Stalin had little or no chance of winning the leadership contest. However, he cunningly persuaded other members of the central committee, especially Kamenev and Zinoviev, to keep the testament secret for the sake of party unity. Moreover, Zinoviev and Kamenev wanted the support of Stalin in stopping Trotsky from becoming leader.

## Lenin's funeral

Stalin successfully presented himself as Lenin's close follower. For example, Stalin appeared as the chief mourner at Lenin's funeral, while Trotsky was conspicuous by his absence. Trotsky was ill and Stalin tricked him into believing the funeral was the previous day. Trotsky was seen as arrogant and disrespectful of Lenin because he could not be bothered to turn up for his funeral. Stalin gave the funeral oration and to onlookers, it seemed as if Stalin was the natural heir to Lenin.

**Source E** From *Leon Trotsky: the Eternal Rebel* by R. Seth published in 1967

*Trotsky was recovering from an illness when Lenin died. He telephoned Stalin to ask when the funeral was to be. Stalin said 'On Saturday, you can't get back in time anyway so we advise you to continue with your treatment.' This was a lie, the funeral was not to be until Sunday and Trotsky could have reached Moscow by then.*

### TASKS

**4** How would Source D help Stalin in his attempts to succeed Lenin?

**5** How far does Source E support the view that Stalin was a devious politician?
(For guidance on answering this type of question, see pages 48–49.)

**Source D** A Photograph showing Stalin (front right) as the chief mourner at Lenin's funeral, 1924

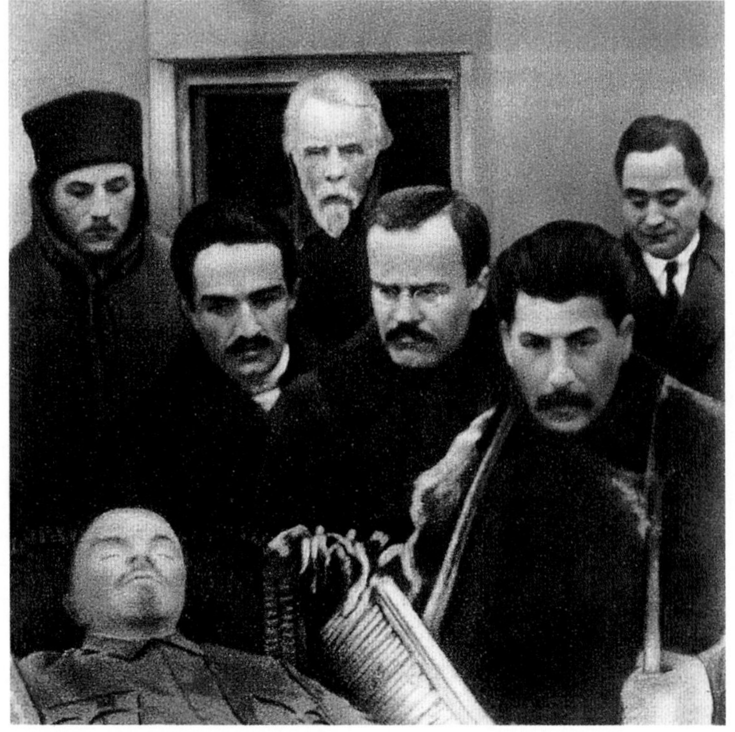

# Why was Stalin favourite to succeed Lenin by the end of 1924?

| **Strengths of Stalin**  | **Weaknesses of Trotsky**  |
|---|---|
| • Most people, especially Trotsky, underestimated Stalin, and saw him only as a boring, unambitious, dull administrator.<br>• Stalin held the key role of general secretary in the Communist Party. He used this position to appoint officials who supported him and he removed known supporters of Trotsky in order to build up a power base within the party. He soon commanded the support of most party officials who owed their position to him.<br>• He carefully built up an image of having been close to Lenin, and, therefore, his natural successor.<br>• He was the chief mourner at Lenin's funeral and made a big speech praising Lenin.<br>• He had photos published showing him at Lenin's side and began to develop the cult of Lenin.<br>• Stalin cleverly played off his rivals against each other. He knew that Kamenev and Zinoviev feared Trotsky and used their support to isolate him.<br>• He began to promote 'Socialism in One Country', which won popular support within the Communist Party because it suggested that the Soviet Union should concentrate on securing communism at home before it supported revolutions abroad. | • Trotsky was seen by many party members as an outsider. This was partly because of his Jewish background, but also because, from 1903 to 1917, he had been a leading **Menshevik**, only changing to the Bolshevik Party in the months before the October Revolution.<br>• He made a series of tactical mistakes and allowed himself to be outmanoeuvred by Stalin. As leader of the Red Army, he had the power to remove his leaders. Instead, he resigned as commander. In addition, he was not prepared to canvass support from his colleagues or rank and file members of the Communist Party.<br>• Trotsky had a superiority complex which upset many of his colleagues. This, in turn, meant that he had little time for intellectual inferiors such as Stalin, whom he seriously underestimated.<br>• He considered Stalin to be average (he called him 'the arch-mediocrity').<br>• Trotsky promoted World Revolution. He wanted the Soviet Union to support Communist revolutions in other countries. However, most Russians preferred to concentrate their resources and energy on fully establishing communism in the Soviet Union. In other words, they preferred 'Socialism in One Country'. |

## TASK

Explain why Stalin emerged as the favourite to succeed Lenin by the end of 1924.
(For guidance on answering this type of question, see page 90.)

# What was Lenin's legacy to Russia?

**Source A** Mourners at Lenin's funeral, Red Square, Moscow, January 1924

Lenin was a true revolutionary. He had sought to remove the Romanovs and the tsarist system and create a true Communist society in Russia. He emerged as the most constant and most determined of the Bolsheviks. He pushed for a second revolution in 1917 and was able to secure the Bolshevik takeover of power.

Lenin's revolution did remove the Romanovs as well as the aristocracy, ***Okhrana***, landowners and the power of the Church. In addition, the revolution had the unintended consequence of driving out about two million people and many of them were the most skilled and educated of the country. Yet with the introduction of the New Economic Policy, Lenin restored some economic stability to Russia by 1924 and the social upheavals of the war and civil war had begun to settle.

**Source B** From *Lenin and the Bolsheviks* by A. Ulam published in 1966

*It must be an indelible stain on Lenin's record that for all his humane instincts he allowed this cult of terror to develop. He allowed mass terror not only to be practised but to become legitimate and respectable.*

**Source C** From an essay written in 1921 by Maxim Gorky, an early supporter of the Bolsheviks and a friend of Lenin. The essay attacked the activities of Lenin after 1918

*Lenin is a gifted man who has all the qualities of a leader including these essential ones: lack of morality, and a merciless, lordly harshness towards the lives of the masses ... As long as I can, I will repeat to the Russian proletariat, you are being led to destruction, you are being used as material in an inhuman experiment; to your leaders, you are not human.*

## TASKS

1 What does Source A show you about Lenin's funeral?
(For guidance on answering this type of question, see page 22.)

2 How far does Source B support the view that Lenin was unconcerned by the suffering of the Russian people in the years 1918–24?
(For guidance on answering this type of question, see pages 48–49.)

3 How useful is Source C to a historian studying the effects of the activities of Lenin?
(For guidance on answering this type of question, see pages 59–60.)

## Lenin: the party leader

From the beginning, Lenin had a clear vision for the Bolshevik Party. He believed in a small, dedicated group of people who would create a revolution and lead the masses to the 'promised land'. For Lenin, the central committee would be the only thinking element in the party and it would make all policies. The committee would direct the development of the party at all times. This frequently created criticism because some wanted to create a broader membership. When war broke out in 1914, Lenin was disgusted by the decision of most socialists in Europe to support the war effort. He opposed Russia's entry into the conflict but hoped it might allow workers in Europe to rebel against their oppressors. He was mistaken – initially.

When he returned to Russia from exile in 1917, he presented not only the party but the Russian people with a clear programme of reform that all could understand. His boundless energy and organisational powers meant that the Bolsheviks were able to overcome even problems such as the July Days (see pages 30–31).

Crucially, he was able to challenge the theories of **Karl Marx** in September and October 1917. He decided to commit Russia to immediate revolution led by the dedicated Bolsheviks without waiting for the bourgeois and proletarian stages that Marx had outlined (see page 27). By doing so Lenin was creating what became known as Marxism–Leninism. It was this adaptation of Marxism which wrong-footed some of the **Socialist Revolutionaries** and Mensheviks.

## Lenin: the leader of Russia

As leader of the first socialist country, Lenin knew he would have to overcome countless difficulties. His use of *Sovnarkom* (see page 42) secured the power of the Bolsheviks in the early days and his ruthlessness in the use of the *Cheka* showed that he was prepared to use any means necessary to maintain power. He believed in the idea of 'the means justifying the end'.

This was made clear when War Communism (see pages 74–75) was adopted during the Civil War. Lenin displayed such ruthlessness in order to maintain the revolution and defeat its enemies. Despite this characteristic, Lenin was also pragmatic. When the Russian economy experienced problems under War Communism, he showed he was not hidebound to political theory by introducing the New Economic Policy. This permitted a measure of private enterprise again and it was a policy that continued for several years after his death.

Lenin quickly ended democracy after the revolution and created a one-party state. He has been criticised for not ensuring a smooth succession. In a state where there was no opposition, a powerful secret police, an all-powerful party and growing terror, the stage was set for a dictator who would take these to their extreme. This was to be Joseph Stalin.

On Lenin's death, Winston Churchill said: 'The Russian people's worst misfortune was his birth; their next worst – his death.'

**Source D** From an article written by Joseph Stalin, first published in *Pravda*, 30 January 1924

*For 25 years Comrade Lenin moulded our party and finally trained it to be the strongest and most highly steeled workers' party in the world. The greatness of Lenin lies above all in this – that by creating the Republic of Soviets he gave a practical demonstration to the oppressed masses of the world that the rule of landlords and capitalists is short-lived. He thus fired the hearts of the workers and peasants of the whole world with the hope of liberation.*

**Source E** From an article in *The Times*, a British newspaper, on 23 January 1924

*Both the Communist Party and Sovnarkom were completely under Lenin's control. It happened sometimes that after listening to a discussion of two conflicting motions in some meeting under his chairmanship, Lenin would dictate to the secretary, without troubling to argue the point, some third resolution which was entirely his own. He had no scruple about methods and treated human beings as mere material for his purpose. The Communist experiment brought Russia to economic ruin, famine and barbarism.*

**Source F** From a letter written by Prince Lvov, first leader of the Provisional Government, to Boris Bakhmeteff, the Provisional Government's ambassador to the USA, November 1923

*The Russian people support Soviet power. That does not mean they are happy with it. But at the same time as they feel their oppression they also see that their own type of people are entering into the apparatus, and this makes them feel that the regime is 'their own'.*

## TASKS

**4** Why do Sources D and E have different views about Lenin's leadership?
(For guidance on answering this type of question, see pages 69–70.)

**5** What does Source F tell you about Russia in 1923?

**6** What did Winston Churchill mean when he said of Lenin: 'The Russian people's worst misfortune was his birth; their next worst – his death.'

**7** Write two obituaries for Lenin. One should be from one of his supporters and one from one of his opponents.

# Examination guidance

This section provides guidance on how to answer an evaluation question from Units 1 and 2. It requires you to make a judgement and discuss why a person, event or development was significant or important.

How important was Stalin's job as General Secretary of the Communist Party in enabling him to succeed Lenin as leader of the USSR? (6 marks)

### Response by candidate

*Stalin's role as General Secretary was very important in enabling him to succeed Lenin as leader of the USSR. It was a key job within the Communist Party which gave him unlimited power to appoint and dismiss individuals. He could appoint officials who supported him and who therefore owed their position directly to him. During 1922-23 he was able to remove known supporters of Trotsky, who was his main rival in the leadership race to succeed Lenin. This helped to strengthen Stalin's power base and considerably weaken support for Trotsky.*

*After Lenin's death Stalin used his position to persuade other members of the Bolshevik Central Committee to keep Lenin's political testament secret as it said that no one person should succeed him. Lenin had wanted a joint leadership. Stalin was able to upstage Trotsky by appearing as the chief mourner in Lenin's funeral and he made a big speech supporting the dead leader. Trotsky had failed to turn up for the funeral but this was because Stalin had deliberately given him the wrong date, and had told him that there was not enough time for him to return to Russia to attend. By not attending, Trotsky was made to look disloyal to Lenin, while Stalin played a leading role in the proceedings.*

*The position of General Secretary was therefore a key role as it provided Stalin with the opportunity to strengthen his support base and weaken that of his main rivals in the leadership race.*

Clear links to the question

Provides specific examples of how Stalin used his job to increase support

A clear judgement which addresses the key issue of 'importance'

## Tips on how to answer

- This question requires you to **evaluate the importance or success** of a particular event, individual, or key issue.
- You must aim to **analyse and evaluate** the reasons for this importance/success.
- Descriptive answers will not score you more than half marks – **you must analyse**.
- You need to support your observations with **specific factual detail**.
- Remember that this question requires you to **provide a judgement**, giving specific reasons why you think this event, individual or issue was important or successful.
- You can, in certain circumstances, **disagree** and argue that the event, individual or issue was not important or successful.

#### Examiner's comment

This is a detailed and well-structured answer. The candidate addresses the key issue throughout and provides several examples to show how the position of General Secretary enabled Stalin to outmanoeuvre his rival Trotsky and succeed Lenin as leader. The concluding sentence provides a judgement and evaluates the importance of Stalin's job as General Secretary. The answer meets the requirements of level 3 and is worthy of receiving the maximum of 6 marks.

### Now you have a go

How important was Lenin's illness in allowing Stalin to grow more powerful within the Communist Party? (6 marks)

## Examination practice

Here is an opportunity for you to practise some of the questions that have been explained in previous chapters.

### Question 1

**a)** What does Source A show you about conditions in Russia in 1921? (2 marks)

**Source A** A starving peasant family during the famine, 1921

- Remember to pick out at least two facts from the picture.
- You must also make use of the information provided in the caption.
- For further guidance, see page 22.

**b)** Use the information in Source B and your own knowledge to explain why there was an uprising at the Kronstadt naval base in March 1921. (4 marks)

**Source B** From a school textbook

*In March 1921 sailors at the Kronstadt naval base staged an uprising because they said that 'life under the Communist dictatorship had become more terrible than death'. These men had been strong supporters of the Bolsheviks during the 1917 revolution but they now felt betrayed. The uprising was put down with extreme force.*

- You will need to pick out at least two facts from the source and explain them in your own words.
- You must demonstrate your knowledge of this topic by providing at least one additional factor not mentioned in the source.
- For further guidance, see page 40.

**c)** How far does Source C support the view that Lenin aimed to suppress religion? (5 marks)

**Source C** Lenin forced thousands of churches to close. In this photograph Communist workers are destroying a monastery

- You must pick out a range of factors from both the picture and the caption, linking them to your own knowledge.
- Remember to give a reasoned judgement which targets the question.
- For further guidance, see pages 48–49.

**d)** How useful is Source D to a historian studying the achievements of Lenin? Explain your answer using the source and your own knowledge. (6 marks)

**Source D** An account which was published on 23 January 1924 in *The Times*, a British newspaper, following the death of Lenin

*Lenin was first and foremost a professional revolutionary. ... This is not the place to describe the terrible achievements of Bolshevism – the shameful peace with Germany, the plundering of the educated and propertied classes, the long continued terror with its thousands of innocent victims ... The Communist experiment brought Russia to economic ruin, famine and barbarism.*

- Aim to concentrate on three focus areas, such as content, origin and purpose.
- Remember to make reference to the usefulness of the source to the historian.
- For further guidance, see pages 59–60.

These two sources say different things about the New Economic Policy.

**e)** Why do Sources E and F have different views about the New Economic Policy? In your answer you should refer both to the content of the sources and to the authors. (8 marks)

**Source E** A report written by Walter Duranty in 1923. He was an American journalist who lived in Russia during the period of the New Economic Policy.

*Living conditions in Russia have enormously improved in the past two years. The essential fact is that everyone is infinitely better off than during the black years of 1920 and 1921 that present conditions seem paradise by comparison. It is estimated that more than 250,000 private traders have moved to Moscow since the NEP began. They crowd the restaurants for dinner with French wines and lose thousands playing cards without turning a hair.*

**Source F** A description of the NEP by Anna Strong which was written in the 1920s. She was a dedicated member of the Communist Party

*In my few short trips into Moscow during the winter of 1921–22, I had been disturbed by the growing private trade. To me each seems a step of defeat ... There's a horrible new rich set growing.*

- You must comment on both sources, in each case making reference to the content and the author.
- Remember to explain why the two sources have different views.
- For further guidance, see pages 69–70.

## Question 2 (from summer 2013 onwards)

**a)** Describe the causes of the Civil War. (4 marks)

- You will need to describe at least two key features.
- Be specific, avoid generalised comments.
- For further guidance, see page 79.

**b)** Explain why the Russian royal family was killed in July 1918. (5 marks)

- Remember to give a variety of reasons.
- Give specific details such as names, dates, events, organisations and activities.
- For further guidance, see page 90.

**c)** How important was the leadership of Trotsky in helping the Reds win the Civil War? (6 marks)

- Remember to evaluate the importance or significance of the named individual, event or issue.
- Remember that this question requires you to provide a judgement giving specific reasons as support.
- You need to support your observations with specific factual detail.
- For further guidance, see page 113.

## Question 3 (from summer 2013 onwards)

Did Lenin's rule from 1921 to 1924 change the lives of the Russian people for the better? (10 marks & 3 marks for SPaG)

In your answer you should:

- discuss aspects of Russian life which improved under Lenin
- discuss aspects of Russian life which did not improve under Lenin.

- Remember to use the advice in the scaffold. It is a useful steer.
- Aim to link your paragraphs, covering a variety of key issues.
- You should provide a conclusion which is linked back to the question.
- For further guidance, see pages 101–2.

**Abdicate** To give up the throne

**Anarchist** Somebody who supports political disorder

**Armistice** An agreement between opposing armies to suspend fighting in order to discuss peace terms

**Arsenals** Stores of weapons

**Atheists** People who do not believe in God

**Autocracy** Rule by one person who has complete power.

**Avant-garde** Pioneers of change in art

**Black market** Illegal trade in goods which are in short supply

**Bolsheviks** A member of one of the groups formed after the split in the Social Democratic Party in 1903. Bolshevik meant majority

**Bourgeois** Member of the middle class

**Cadets** A political party founded in 1906. It wanted a constitutional monarchy and an elected parliament

**Central Powers** The collective name given to Germany, Austria-Hungary, Turkey and Bulgaria in the First World War

***Cheka*** The Bolsheviks' secret police

**Comintern** Short for 'Communist International' – international organisation based in Russia, formed to assist the growth of communism all over the world

**Commissar** Term for government minister

**Constituent Assembly** Assembly or parliament elected in November 1917 to draw up a new constitution for Russia. The Assembly met briefly in January 1918

**Cossacks** People of southern Russia, Ukraine, and Siberia, noted for their horsemanship and military skill

***Coup d'état*** Violent or illegal change of government

**Dictatorship** System of government where the ruler is not restricted by a constitution, laws or any opposition

**Dual Power** The term used to describe the balance of power between the Provisional Government and the Petrograd Soviet

***Duma*** The Russian word for parliament

**Food requisitioning** Seizing produce

**Guerrilla** A person who fought in small groups against conventional forces, using such methods as sabotage and ambush

***Gulag*** Prison where inmates were punished by forced labour

**Haemophilia** Hereditary disease that prevents the blood from clotting during bleeding. Even a minor cut could lead to excessive bleeding and death

**Hedonistic** Indulging in sensual pleasures

**Karl Marx** German political theorist who wrote *The Communist Manifesto* (1848) and *Das Kapital* (1867)

***Komsomol*** The Communist youth movement

***Kulaks*** The name given to the better-off peasants who had benefited from Lenin's New Economic Policy. From selling their produce, these peasants became more well-off than other peasants and began to employ poorer peasants to work for them

**Left wing** The more radical members of a political party

**Mensheviks** A member of one of the groups formed after the split in the Social Democratic Party in 1903. They believed the party should be a mass organisation, which all workers could join

**Military Revolutionary Committee (MRC)** A body originally set up by Socialist Revolutionaries and the Social Democrats to defend against Germany and counter-revolution

**Monarchism** A system of government in which the country is ruled by a king or queen

**Nepmen** Merchants/traders who became rich due to the New Economic Policy

**New Economic Policy (NEP)** Introduced in 1921 by Lenin to win back support of people. Allowed private businesses and farms and profit

**October Manifesto** Issued by Tsar Nicholas II in 1905. This promised constitutional reforms and he hoped it would end the unrest of that year

**Octobrists** Members of the political party favouring constitutional reforms granted in the manifesto issued by Nicholas II in 1905

***Okhrana*** The tsarist secret police

**Orthodox Church** Branch of Christianity, strong in Eastern Europe, established by a breakaway from the Catholic Church in the early middle ages

**Party line** The policies of a political party which all members are expected to follow

***Pravda*** The official Communist Party newspaper

**Proletariat** The industrial working class

***Proletkult*** Combined Russian words meaning proletarian culture

**Provisional Government** Temporary government set up after the abdication of Tsar Nicholas II

**Red Guard** The Bolsheviks' own armed forces

**Red Terror** The period of *Cheka* repression under the Bolsheviks

**Republicanism** Support for an elected government with a president

**Russification** The policy of forcing non-Russians such as Poles to speak Russian and follow Russian customs

**Secretariat** A form of civil service that carried out the administration policies

**Separatists** Supporters of states who wanted to be independent of Russia

**Socialist Realism** The official art form under Stalin which was supposed to show the life of peasants and workers but was used to glorify Stalin and his achievements

**Socialist Revolutionaries (SRs)** A major political party in Russia in the early twentieth century. They believed in a revolution of the peasants and wanted to remove the tsar

**Soviet** An elected council of workers

***Sovnarkom*** The Council of People's Commissars or the government of Russia

**Tundra** Huge treeless zone stretching from Arctic Russia to the treeline. It has a permanently frozen sub-soil

**USSR** Union of Soviet Socialist Republics. The name given to Russia in 1922

**Utopian Communist state** A state where citizens work freely for the sake of everyone else, using their own abilities to the best advantage of society

***Vesenkha*** Supreme Council of National Economy which controlled industry

**War Communism** State control of industry and agriculture

**Western Front** During the First World War, 1914–1918, the 'Western Front' referred to a series of trench lines that ran from the Belgian coast to the Alps

***Zhenotdel*** The name given to the women's department in the Communist Party